Bicycle Highway

BICYCLE HIGHWAY

*Celebrating Community
Radio in Ireland*

Edited by
Rosemary Day

The Liffey Press

Published by
The Liffey Press
Ashbrook House, 10 Main Street,
Raheny, Dublin 5, Ireland
www.theliffeypress.com

© 2007 Rosemary Day
and individual contributors

A catalogue record of this book is
available from the British Library.

ISBN 978-1-905785-37-7

Printed in Ireland by Colour Books

Contents

Part 3 – Personal Reflections

This book is dedicated to all of the people who make community radio happen in Ireland

1

Introduction: Community Radio, What Could Be Simpler?

Rosemary Day

It's a summer's day and I'm freewheeling along, passing all the traffic that's backed up to God knows where. I'm getting where I want to go and I'm enjoying the ride. My bike won't take me all around the world today but I don't want to go there, I just want to get around my home town. My bike cost me very little to buy, it's actually second hand and quite old. It costs nothing to run – just a bit of energy and the belief that if I keep pushing I'll get there. Sometimes I cycle on the road with the cars and trucks. Other times I can go up on the pavement or off down a boreen that takes my fancy. I'm free, I go at my own pace; I meet up with others. We wave, sometimes we stop and chat or we travel together for a while. I'm not alone. I know there are many others cycling along like me, all over the country and throughout the world.

What is a bicycle highway and what does it have to do with community radio in Ireland? Community radio is a movement which seeks to build the communities from which it springs and which it serves. It does this by depending on the members of those communities to do it themselves. That means volunteers who work for no money and often on old equipment costing them little or no money at all. So the analogy of the bicycle is a useful one. In the days of high-tech gizmos, the information highway and motorways built to deliver people, goods and services at high speeds, the very notion of a bicycle highway may seem an anachronism. However, we find today that the bicycle is a useful way to get around in cities, often quicker than in cars or by public transport. The bicycle is cheap to buy and to run. Using it makes a person healthier and protects the environment – it is ecologically sound. It may not be great for getting you across the entire country or for transnational travel, but for getting around in your own neighbourhood there is little to beat it. In the last few years in Ireland we see second-hand bicycles in use by new immigrants, by the ecologically aware, by the well educated and affluent, by the young and by the active retired – much like community radio. A highway is designed to connect people and places directly and speedily, without obstruction or delay. Community radio connects people in communities with the minimum of mediation; the people speak to themselves, immediately and effectively.

Community radio is cheap, accessible and it works well in a small space or for a small group. Why have a digital platform that can reach millions and costs you millions when you only want to reach 10,000 people? Community radio is small-scale and easy to use. Radio is the first broadcasting medium, but it still works. Despite the rise of iPods and MP3 players, radio is the most widely-used broadcasting medium in Ireland today. It is the medium of unconscious choice and of inconspicuous consumption. The reach of community radio is also wider than that of newer technologies. Listening to the radio does not require computer literacy or indeed any type of literacy, it is truly a basic medium. To hear a radio programme does not require broadband, a PC or any special training. Most households in Ireland have several radios – in different rooms, in cars and in tiny portable forms. Radio costs so little for the listener and for the broadcaster that like the humble bicycle we often take it for granted.

That forum became the representative association known to-day as CRAOL, responsible for sponsoring this book. Nessa McGann, former chairperson, takes up the story of Irish commu-nity radio from 1998 to the present day in Chapter 4, "From a Forum to a Force: The Development of CRAOL, 1998-2007". She discusses the development of the community radio movement in Ireland into a cohesive force for networking, lobbying, training and development.

Part Two, "Aims and Issues", looks at the aims, issues and main concerns of community radio in Ireland today. Each chapter explores an area of major importance for community radio activ-ists and uses the example of one or more of Ireland's community radio stations to show how these issues are approached in prac-tice. In Chapter 5, "Community Radio and Community Develop-ment", Rosemary Day assesses the value of working in a commu-nity development manner for community radio stations.

Chapter 6, "Empowerment through Community Radio: NEAR Fm as an Example", describes some of the strategies employed to ensure the meaningful participation of marginalised groups in a community radio station. Introduced by Jack Byrne, the chapter explores what empowerment means in a community radio sta-tion. Ciarán Murray and Sally Galliano of NEAR Fm and the Dub-lin Media Co-op draw on their experiences as station and project managers in the North East of Dublin city to bring us a variety of examples of the empowerment process at work, ranging from recently released prisoners to immigrants newly arrived in the country.

Ensuring the inclusion of women from all walks of life and at all levels of production and management is a priority for commu-nity radio activists who work to bring those who are marginalised into the communication process. Nessa McGann, former station manager of Wired Fm, now Programme Director of Spin 103, draws on her postgraduate research to provide us with examples of how this is accomplished in two Irish community radio stations,

NEAR Fm and Radio Corca Baiscinn, in Chapter 7, "Women in Irish Community Radio".

Chapter 8, "Adult Education through Community Radio: The Example of Community Radio Castlebar", describes how community radio can be the ideal vehicle to deliver adult education. Pat Stanton, Mayo VEC's Adult Education Officer and one of the founders of Community Radio Castlebar, describes their innovative and successful adult literacy project.

Specific programming can fit the needs of particular target groups in a community. The former Irish language officer of the BCI, now the Chief Executive of the Independent Broadcasters of Ireland (IBI), Lisa Ní Choisdealbha, describes the work done through the community radio sector to bring programmes in the Irish language to fluent Irish speakers and to learners of the language in Chapter 9, "An Ghaeilge agus an Raidió Pobail: The Irish Language and Community Radio".

Chapter 10, "Student Community Radio", looks at communities of a different kind, those of students who broadcast to themselves on campus-based stations in Ireland. Catríona Chambers, station manager of Cork Campus Radio, describes this specific community, its needs and its ambitions and gives examples from the three student community radio stations: FLIRT, based in Galway, Wired Fm in Limerick and Cork Campus Radio in her native city of Cork.

The final chapter in Part Two, Chapter 11, "Support for Community Radio", looks at two important concerns for all community radio stations – finance and training. BCI officers Stephanie Comey and Margaret Tumelty describe the sources of funding throughout the entire sector and give an overview of the development of training programmes in Irish community radio stations over a 12-year period.

Part Three, "Personal Reflections", is a delightful freewheel down memory lane. People who have been working in Irish community radio stations, some since the 1970s, get the chance to reminisce about their lives as community radio activists and in the process they showcase their own home stations. Noel Cronin was one of the founders of the very first community radio station in Ireland, Community Radio Youghal, or CRY as it has always been known. He describes the thrills and the promise of the pirate days on the coast of East Cork in Chapter 12, "CRY in the Afternoon: The Early Days in Youghal".

In a similar vein, Mike Purcell, veteran of the oldest Dublin community radio station, Dublin South Community Radio (DSCR), provides a lively description of the trials, tribulations and triumphs of Dublin's very first community radio station in Chapter 13, "Community Radio Memories: Dublin South Fm".

In Chapter 14, "Raidió na Life: Raidió na Réabhlóide", Fachtna Ó Drisceoil reflects on the contribution Ireland's only Irish language community radio station has made to the Irish language revival, to the mass media in general and to his own career as a broadcaster in RTÉ in particular. This chapter is written in Irish with a short summary in English for those who are not fluent in the language.

The early days of Ireland's smallest community radio station, Connemara Community Radio, are described by their first station manager, Mary Ruddy, in Chapter 15, "Dialogue Not Monologue: Connemara Community Radio". A strong force in the Irish community radio movement and a former member of the AMARC Europe General Council and of the IRTC, Mary also reflects on community radio as a movement and stresses the importance of the relationship between the station and all of the members of its community. The current station manager, Pat Walshe, captures the breadth of experience which this tiny rural station in North Connemara has garnered in his description of their Outside Broadcasting Unit at the end of the chapter.

In Chapter 16, "Agitate, Educate, Organise: Dundalk Fm100", Alan Byrne recalls the difficulties of getting a community radio station started, the help received along the way and the development of the station today.

Jim Doherty and Jimmy McBride introduce us to the most northerly station, Raidió Pobail Inis Eoghain, in Chapter 17, "Northern View: Raidió Pobail Inis Eoghain". They recall the usual ups and downs of getting started but infuse their story with the particular difficulties experienced by a border community on an isolated peninsula. Never ones to whinge, however, their story is one of the joys of working collaboratively to build a community and with it a fine community radio station.

Ciarán Ryan, former Training and Development Officer with West Limerick Community Radio, gives us an insight into what is involved in preparing a station for its first days on air in the final chapter, "Going on Air: West Limerick 102".

As this book goes to print there are 21 licensed community radio stations on air in Ireland, with more expected to follow shortly. The representative association of community radio stations in Ireland, CRAOL, works as a network but also as a resource to its members and to groups who are thinking of setting up their own community radio stations. If you want to go beyond the experience of reading about community radio in Ireland, if you feel your community would benefit from having its own station, make contact with CRAOL today on www.craol.ie and join us on the Bicycle Highway.

PART ONE

History

2

If Community Radio is the Answer . . . What is the Question? The Birth of Community Radio in Ireland, 1975–1995

Jack Byrne

My introduction to the power of media to influence attitude and behaviour came as I and others tried to establish a communally-owned consumers' co-operative in the late 1970s. We tried to encourage local people to see the empowering value of buying from their own retail outlet but we struggled to compete with full-page advertising from our commercial rivals as we had only a creaking Gestetner printing machine. Even though the co-op was cheaper than the local supermarkets for a full shopping basket, the allure of an exciting full-page ad, offering a halfpenny, or even tuppence, off selected items, was too strong to resist and our venture collapsed, starved of media oxygen.

During this dark period I heard the sound of the many pirate radio stations emerging across Dublin city and I saw a way to fight back. We could have our own communally-owned radio station to promote community development initiatives. The ideas were poorly formed, but evolving. Around then, I met with John Murphy and Sally Reynolds of Bray Local Broadcasting, BLB. They were already doing it. And Tom Murchan, Tony Duggan and Mike Purcell from the Churchtown Residents' Association, who were also interested in using radio for community development. As we met and talked and called public meetings, we were joined by others, John Conroy from Tallaght and Dave Tobin from Finglas. Gentlemen all, you'll have noticed, with the honourable exception of Sally. But then the radio scene in the late 1970s was awash with testosterone, strutting male DJs with big medallions and even larger egos.

The radio scene was also in flux. The Wireless Telegraphy Bill 1979 was circulated. It proposed to close all pirates. They responded by attempting to collaborate in defence of their right to broadcast. But it proved impossible to get so much self-importance to co-operate. By contrast, the nascent community radio movement began to organise a lobby and to discuss the principles of community broadcasting. We were joined by Brian Reynolds and Fr. Brian Molloy from the Catholic Communications Centre in Booterstown, and by people from Tipperary, Kerry and Kilkenny. In the latter case, by Fr. Jerry Joyce, a very articulate and able defender of community radio.

For my part, in north-east Dublin we lobbied at least 50 local community organisations to attend a meeting on the matter. I booked a room in the Camelot Hotel and rushed up from work in Wexford on the night in question to lay out the 50 chairs and stood ready at the podium. And there I was, with no one to speak to. No one showed up. Daunted, dismayed but undeterred, I delivered my prepared words of wisdom and empowerment to the empty chairs. I'm sure you'll agree that from such a position the only way was up!

Shortly after, I was joined by Vincent Teeling, a young man who understood how technical things worked. He ought to have, he had practiced for years on everything mechanical that his poor mother bought. Also, Dave O'Connor and Tomás Mac Ruairí, Michael Farrell, Noreen Byrne, Brendan Teeling, Derek Ó Broin and Tríona Nic Ruairí. These were the main group who established our radio co-operative in the early 1980s.

The Broadcasting and Wireless Telegraphy Bill 1980 and the Independent Radio Authority Bill 1981 came and went to the shredder, without making any impact on the pirate scene. There were now a credible number of stations subscribing to notions of non-commercial radio. Some even flirted with democratic ownership. However, there was still no clear definition of community radio. This led to many with suspect agendas edging into the community radio sector. I found that quite often, in talking to "suits" who liked the notion of volunteering – that is, people working for nothing in radio – they usually balked at the idea of actually being non-profit making. I recall that as the old AM, medium wave technology was being superseded by FM transmission, some politicians mused that maybe communities could be allowed onto this AM band. We were being offered dominance on a largely defunct system, while being deprived of access to the increasingly popular FM band. Restraining people's access to knowledge is a common disempowerment strategy.

Nowadays we are fortunate here in Ireland that we have a good working relationship with the Broadcasting Commission of Ireland (BCI, previously the Independent Radio and Television Commission, IRTC). There is a commitment to the development of existing services and to the emergence of further community radio services so that there is no strategy to deprive people of access to media ownership. We need to build on this and position our community media sector to take advantage of the next technological shift from analogue to digital delivery systems. However, back in the 1980s, realising what we were up against in terms of duplicity, opportunism and incomprehension, those of us concerned with keeping the sector focused decided that we needed to form an association and write up some operating principles. In 1983, the National Association of Community Broadcasting (NACB) was founded. It drew up a set of principles, not unlike the AMARC Europe Charter (see appendix) now familiar to Irish community stations. AMARC is the French acronym for the

World Association of Community Radio Broadcasters and Irish community radio activists have a proud and productive history of involvement with it. Our first chair was Tomás Roseingrave of Muintir na Tíre. Already there was a community development instinct within the group.

In 1985, the NACB came within a whisker of securing legislation which would have established a community radio sector, based on the co-operative model. Two parties, Labour and Fine Gael, were in government as a coalition, and Labour favoured community-based stations with RTÉ involvement, while Jim Mitchell, Minister for Communications, wanted to bring in commercial, local radio. Mervyn Taylor, Labour Party TD, invited six of us into the Dáil on the eve of a crucial debate on this bill which had struggled for some 18 months through tortuous wrangling between the Labour and Fine Gael partners. I recall that we took over the Senate room and phoned all of the Labour TDs in the building to secure their support for the bill, as we recognised that it was as good a compromise as we were likely to get. We spent the entire evening meeting with Labour TDs in corridors and the bar, discussing the merits of the bill. At about two o'clock in the morning (don't tell me that TDs knock off early) we achieved a compromise bill which would have secured community radio in a two-tier system, which Jim Mitchell had conceded, in order to get his bill through. Of course, it would also make provision for commercial, local radio as the other tier and many Labour deputies still had difficulties with this. The bill stalled again and fell with the coalition government a short time later. Our association sat waiting for a new government and with it came the arrival of Fianna Fáil Minister Ray Burke. Who said things were looking up?

With the establishment of the 1988 Sound Broadcasting Act, Minister Burke told us that he was going to licence the commercial stations first and that after a short interval the community stations could have their turn. We'd have to promise, of course, not to upset the apple cart for the serious radio players. We might have to take a vow of poverty. He also advised that he was intent on introducing "light touch" legislation. Which was correct: we felt nothing for almost six years, until Michael D. Higgins, Labour TD, became Minister for Arts, Culture and the Gaeltacht. This was a significant change of emphasis. The government department charged with overseeing broadcasting had moved from Posts and Telegraphs, through Communications and now to Culture, so that human communication was now seen as a cultural imperative. Of course, it moved away from this notion later with the creation of Arts, Heritage and the Gaeltacht, under Fianna Fáil Minister Síle De Valera.

While we were chagrined at having to sit on the sidelines, with hindsight I believe that the IRTC inadvertently did us a favour. Many of the advocates of community radio at that time had a very limited view of the potential of alternative radio. Most were set on offering a model not unlike that now offered by local radio, that is, a mainly music diet interspersed with local ads. So that once this model was on air across the country, courtesy of local commercial radio, we had to sit back and ask ourselves why were we still seeking licences when the commercials had stolen our clothes? Was there yet another way to do radio that was qualitatively different? Luckily there was – it meant devising a more accessible format, one that allowed participants to appropriate their radio station and to gain confidence in being media practitioners. To some of us, it meant devising a deeper model of communication than had heretofore been available to Irish audiences.

Right through this period, the problem was what to do with a community radio station once you got one. Those seeking licences differed widely. Some proponents still felt that to play local requests and sell advertising to local business was sufficient. Others saw the issue more as one of scale. To be successful, they opined, the station needed to cover a large area to sell advertising to even more businesses. Some of us felt that there wasn't much point in all of this voluntary effort in order to create a commercial station, similar to the locals, whatever the size. Almost all of us felt that our role was to fill the niche between public service and commercial media, providing whatever type of service was missing.

During this period of the late 1980s and early 1990s, we experimented with a whole range of ideas from democratic access to diversity of content to community development, without having the language to define them. None of us were reading Habermas or Chomsky at this early stage. Some of us were reading our near neighbour Peter Lewis and others had even heard of Stuart Hall. But we were instinctively putting into practice notions of a cultural space and diversity, of democratic technics and the establishment of a countervailing force to globalised, commercial media. We worked on the basis that this felt right and that we'd figure it out later. I think that this is a process still unfolding within Irish community radio.

Around this time, we were planning the fourth AMARC international community radio conference, which was to be held in Dublin in August 1990. Bruce Girard, a worldly-wise aficionado of community radio, came to Ireland to help us, as he had been involved with organising previous AMARC conferences. I arranged for Bruce to conduct a workshop around his experiences in Canada, where the idea of a limited form of sponsorship and a clear definition of community radio as democratic and not-for-profit had emerged. Some of those at the workshop liked his ideas, especially me, while others still hankered after a more commercial model. I still hear echoes of that debate in the CRAOL network today.

Just as an afterthought, let me tell you that when we got our licence and NEAR Fm came on air, we adapted the Canadian sponsorship model and years later Bruce enquired about how it was going. I said it was reasonably successful and he replied that this was interesting, as it hadn't worked in Canada! Go figure, as our North American friends would say.

Mention of the AMARC conference leads me to recall the cynical behaviour of the Commission of the IRTC at that time. Just before the arrival of the international delegates, the IRTC published an advertisement in the national dailies asking for expressions of interest in community radio services. Yet, within months of the departure of the international community radio people, the IRTC could announce that it had decided to postpone the process of licensing and would embark on an extensive study of the sector, in spite of the fact that everybody on the planet who knew anything about community radio had just been in Dublin and none of them had been invited into the Commission for a chat.

Worse was to follow. The same Commission then decided to establish one city-wide station which would be offered to some of the applicants for licences across Dublin. At the time I described it as a dustbin – a dustbin into which the commission proposed to fling everyone, from local geographic communities or parishes to Irish speakers and religious groups, any and all groups which the IRTC appeared to consider to be trouble makers and clearly not committed to the respectable pursuit of profit. The successful applicants were not to call the project "community", as presumably this term was giving the Commission heartburn. Eventually, this project was established and the collateral damage was a fractious disintegration of the NACB.

Then, as I mentioned earlier, along came Labour Minister Michael D. Higgins. Minister Higgins appointed a new Commission, which included Mary Ruddy from Connemara Community Radio (see Chapter 15) and Jude Bowles, from the Combat Poverty Agency, with Niall Stokes, the editor of *Hot Press*, a popular music magazine, as its chair. This commission had the vision to see the potential of democratic, not-for-profit radio. Luckily, this initiative from the Minister was met by the remnants of community radio activism on the ground. It was decided by the Commission to establish a pilot project involving 11 community radio stations. Ten of these survived and they established the foundations of a vibrant community radio network across the state.

During the period we called "dead air", when we were sitting on the sidelines, we had identified two types of community radio: those associated with a geographical location and those to serve a community of interest. The definitions still left a great deal to local interpretation. Much of the final model was thrashed out during what could be termed the "Athlone Convention" and was then ratified at the "Shieling Accord" when the Community Radio Forum met at the Old Shieling Hotel in Sutton in Dublin (see Chapter 3). This "Community Radio Model for Ireland" was forwarded to the IRTC in 1997 and now forms the basis of the Commission's policy and practice in licensing community radio. The group who devised proposals in Athlone included the late Tom Murchan of Dublin South Community Radio (see Chapter 13), who gave many decades of his life to the development of community radio.

This is the story of a journey that was marked by incomprehension, both by the community activists and the legislators. But it is also a tale of stubborn determination to clarify what democratic technics might look like in practice, what genuine access to media could provide and how such a model might deliver an entirely different form of communication. We came to realise that we were not, after all, filling a niche between public service and commercial media. We were creating an entirely new space for citizens to appropriate their media in the name of a more participatory democracy.

We have arrived at this point due to the innovative work of the first community radio stations; they laid the foundation for all that is now and will follow later. I tip my hat to my colleagues in the aforementioned stations and say, "Well done!"

During the time prior to the pilot licensing period, the "dead air" time, and during the pilot phase itself, we discussed what in fact we were trying to do in agitating for a third media sector. We tried to articulate innate urges during this time of reflection and some of us made significant progress in our perceptions, and indeed in the development of our philosophy of community radio. Some of these reflections are now offered.

Community building was one topic we kept returning to. We sensed that urban community radio would have a more difficult task than either campus or rural radio is establishing itself. Generally, there is not the same sense of cohesion within an urban setting, particularly in large cities such as Dublin. This has been the case, but the experience of urban community radio has been that those stations that saw themselves more as community building projects and less as radio stations have been more successful in integrating themselves into their communities. They did not unnerve community activists with media jargon, but instead engaged with their community around development issues. It became clear to us, as we identified the main components of community radio, that they bore a striking resemblance to those defined as being at the core of community development work. Tasks such as collective actions, advancing equality, empowerment and participation, promoting social inclusion, emphasising process as well as product are of primary importance in community development projects and in community radio stations (see Chapter 5). I'd like to think that by now, most community radio practitioners see their station as firmly within the broad definition of community building, rather than as radio stations, which operate to make a profit. We have become development specialists and our speciality is the medium of radio as a communal resource. There is now, I'm pleased to say, a strong relationship between many community stations and community activists generally across Ireland.

Not surprisingly, as we were focused on radio programming, content has always been the most contentious area of debate. Some felt that a radio service named after the locality and playing a range of music and airing local advertising was sufficient. I recall that we had endless discussions around this idea of a greater diversity of content and what it might mean in reality. Some held that "diversity of content" should be interpreted conservatively as providing a service of music and of interviews that are not aired on the local commercial stations. The reality which community radio activists must face is a multi-faceted one. Each community station is faced with a spectrum of listeners with a multiplicity of tastes and needs to be met. Clearly, part of the programme mix should be to service existing needs, but that could be to act as no more than a weather vane for fads, many of which would be generated by the more powerful commercial mass media. Some of us felt that a community service could be much more. We argued that while not all community stations may be linked to alleviating local disadvantage, or seeking to raise awareness of global issues, they all should be united in seeking to reflect a community voice, not dictated by either commercial or state interests.

This, of course, raised a further question: was it realistic to consider involving every citizen in media? But, of course, every one of us is already engaged in media. We are surrounded by "facts", we *are* all reporters, each one of us handles large amounts of data in a systematic way every day, receiving and analysing, selecting and recounting. It is only a small step to move from our present position, we argued, to one in which we become more active participants in data flow, shaping and influencing at fundamental levels the information in the media system. This was clearly a different role for participants and would require a very different form of radio service. In order to challenge inequalities in power and information, we needed to understand not only the language and the processes of the media, but also how the media are developing and adjusting to economic and political change. Being on the inside, we sensed that being part of the process would make it easier to understand the current media situation and enable us to begin developing our own language, concepts and strategies.

The existence of a community radio service in a locality could provide people with an alternative range of ideas. It would promote popular participation, which would assist the emergence of a more participative democracy. We could use our communally-owned media to call for a reconstructed democracy, committed to widespread citizen participation in the protection of public information.

Some of us sensed these things and we worked for them and now community radio is a reality, but one still in a quite confused state, not unlike the wider community. A scattered, distracted populace has little opportunity or time to debate long-term environmental or economic threats. Commercial media have little interest in non-commercial matters, so it falls to community radio to provide the town hall, the market square, the *agora* or the public forum for people to define themselves, to construct their own identities and to decide together how to deal with issues of interest or concern.

If a local community wants to retain an autonomous cultural space and to empower itself with relevant information in order to resist economic and environmental impacts, then the local struggle is not enough. The struggle must go beyond the local boundaries and must link with similar communities facing similar problems. Heretofore, it was not very easy for such solidarity and joint actions, but now, with the globe-spanning abilities of information technology, a local community can make these connections. Commercial operators are not the only ones who can go global. It should not be the role of community radio to define people in their locality, but it may be useful for a community radio service to provide the space for ongoing dialogue around these issues. It may even be proper to initiate and sustain this dialogue as a public service. Perhaps the role of community radio is to facilitate people, on air, to draw attention to a danger or a trend and then allow people themselves to decide what to do. Whether local people ever get these alternative perspectives and these broadcast opportunities depends on the local community radio activists.

This developmental approach to the medium, we sensed, and I firmly believe, has been proven right. It has had a beneficial impact on the type of programmes broadcast on Irish community radio stations. Rather than modelling themselves on commercial radio formats, or even on the many excellent RTÉ public service programmes, those community radio stations, seeing themselves as being more in the community and voluntary sector and less in the radio sector, have had to devise entirely novel approaches to content. This dynamic is still being worked through. Seeking less to mediate their community and more to allow access to individuals and community organisations to tell their own stories has meant that such community stations have had to experiment with alternative methods of training and essentially different production values. We realised, very early on, that existing media training modules were inadequate to the needs of an alternative media. We felt that we were developing a different type of medium and that everything about it should change. Our different goals and structures oblige us to establish more suitable methodologies. We need to develop within the movement our own core of alternatively experienced trainers and to develop more participative modes of learning (see Chapters 4 and 11). Our difference gives us the freedom to follow different goals and in a different manner. I believe that this perception and these practices are now well established within the Irish community radio movement.

Funding has always presented problems. We anticipated that a rural or small town community radio station could quickly establish a profile in their locality, whereas urban community radio stations generally have an identity problem and are less likely to be sponsored or supported commercially by local business. Again, the more successful community stations have moved themselves out of the commercial advertising sector and into the community actions category. The more successful community stations, starting from a position where they met official incomprehension, are now in a position to lobby for quite lucrative grants. This type of programme-led funding is ideal for the further development of authentic community radio. With a successful model for community radio now a reality, the BCI can confidently offer this resource to the many communities across the state. Community development radio and allied IT streaming of content will provide the community and voluntary sector with an invaluable tool to advance its work.

I recall that the debate about the importance of commercial or community development funding was still raging when we met in Youghal, for a Forum meeting of the stations involved in the IRTC pilot scheme, some years back in 1996. I was trying to convince people that moving away from advertising and towards public grants to make community development-type programmes would pay dividends. My mantra for the weekend was, "We're not radio stations, we're community development projects, who use radio as a tool." It was a long mantra, but I sensed a swing that weekend towards the latter model. I must confess that it was not my brilliant oratory which swayed them, but the fact that I mentioned that radio advertising was then generating around £50 million annually, while public grants were running at £600 million per annum. Community radio people may be many things, but they are not stupid. During the pilot period, there was a perceptible shift in terminology and aspirations. The notion of community building was growing and that of radio commercialism was waning ... in the main.

I have always believed that community radio can carve out a significant role for itself in the area of media literacy and appropriation. By "media literacy" I mean the ability to evaluate and produce effective communication, and "appropriation" signifies the citizens' assumption of control of both media institutions and of their contents. If people are to be effective in appropriating their media, then they need to become critically aware of how media are organised, how they function, how their content impacts on individuals and cultures, and how their contents might be analysed and utilised for progressive purposes.

Media literacy is the critical first step, because people, young and old, spend so much of their time consuming media content, little realising that it is they who are being swallowed. To shield themselves, people will need to develop a critical appreciation of these issues, and if they wish to be effective media practitioners then they will also need to master these media techniques. People can't begin to appropriate their media effectively without first obtaining a firm grasp of how current media function.

"Media appropriation", in practice, means empowerment, in the sense that it enables people to participate in the processes of public communication, to understand and resist the manipulation of most media content and to devise their own media content. Such an appropriation of their media by people is an essential step in the development of a more participatory democracy, both political and economic. Widespread media literacy and control is essential if individuals are to exercise the power of awareness, to make rational decisions and to become effective citizens. In a world where several media moguls seem set to control all global media output, we should be aware of what we have acquired and the opportunities that lie before us. Neither commercial nor public service media have the scope to experiment, as we have. We have in our grasp opportunities for genuinely public systems and real citizen involvement. We need to explore just where these freedoms can lead us. The fact that a media service exists in the control of citizens in a locality is a significant event.

We should not underestimate the importance, however meagre, the present output may be from such services. The democratic existence and the radical potential of community media are the important factors right now. With encouragement and practice, people can become competent media practitioners as they converse within a secured cultural space about issues that really matter to them. However, the potential can be wasted if such alternative services end up aping mainstream media, attitudes and content. Media literacy will need to address these concerns, will need to alert people to the wasted potential of following the dominant models.

Media literacy and media appropriation are a combination of tactics that deal with *how* to do media and *why* to do media *differently*.

Most of us in community radio realise that both the small things and the big issues are important. In community radio, we find that people respond well to the small, the local. They respond to those things they know about and can expect to influence. Community radio can show local citizens how they can also exert an influence over those global, apparently intractable, issues. A community station can best do this by linking to the global movement of progressive communication.

This is not a betrayal of the local. Environmental issues, global economics, human rights across the planet, all impact on the locality where a community station exists. In order to offer a full service to its listeners, a community station must engage with these wider topics. In the context of the growing influence of global mass communications, we need to examine how a small community station, even when linked to a national network such as CRAOL, can protect the local culture while influencing the global dynamic. Most community stations feel that they have enough to do to deal with the local space, but by adopting this narrow approach no adequate countervailing power is developing to withstand the global commercial communicator. As with any small, isolated project, such isolation leaves the project always vulnerable to hostile action or the vagaries of chance. Solidarity and mutuality are not just slogans. They can have a real value for each community station, leading to support, advice and networked strength.

As a matter of self-interest, each community station should devote some time and energy to developing the national network, CRAOL (see chapter 4), and to encouraging that network to forge active links with the international community radio movement, AMARC. The European section was largely developed at the AMARC 4 conference in UCD in Dublin in 1990, and some of us played a prominent part in negotiating the AMARC Community Radio Charter for Europe (see appendix) which was ratified in Slovenia in 1994.

Listeners to a community radio station live their lives in a limited time and space; it has become increasingly difficult to separate this local from a global dynamic. Today economic and political structures connect the local to the global. This interconnection means that decisions made by the World Bank in Washington affect the lives and environments of millions across the planet. Decisions made in Wall Street to move an industry from the west of Ireland to Eastern Europe can have a devastating effect on a locality. We argued in the 1980s, and still contend, that community radio stations which do not link their locality to the global issues do their local listeners a disservice. Yet it would be wrong to assume that all globalised forms are without progressive possibilities. The problem at present is that most of our media explain all such developments within a capitalist logic, collapsing all other potentials without debate. Faced with the commercial globalisation of media, we have no alternative but to develop a global dimension for democratic media, in policy, ideology and practice. We need a more vigorous aspiration, one that seeks to wrest back control over content, ownership and the ultimate purpose of the electronic global commons. While democratic media is essentially local in outlook, it needs to be global in aspiration, using information technology to link the villages of the world.

If we set ourselves this task, what do we face? For a start, commercial media have a clear set of characteristics and assumptions that espouse consumption as the key to personal fulfilment, and that laud the free market as the bastion of individual liberty. All such media, even as they compete, co-operate in supporting the market ideology. In contrast, community media groups are very often isolated from each other with relatively few interactions and exchanges, which is odd, as they are not competitors and almost all understand the value of co-operation. We operate in this fractured way because we don't yet share an ideology, although I'm sure that virtually all community media would find it easy to agree on the main components of such an ideology. I believe we would serve the cause of democratic media and civil society well if we could begin the task of devising these principles. For a start, we need to explore with civil society what our espousing of "the right to communicate" implies. In case you are wondering what this "right" is, I refer you to the very first line of the AMARC Europe Charter, which is attached by the BCI to the contract for a broadcast licence of every community radio station. It says that:

> Community radios, promote the right to communicate, assist the free flow of information and opinions, encourage creative expression and contribute to the democratic process and a pluralist society. (See appendix.)

The right to communicate is more than the sum of the existing rights; those of freedom to impart information, and the freedom to receive it, or have access to it. It goes beyond information itself, to establish a right to create dialogue, and therefore goes beyond the merely interactive nature of much of current media. It asserts the right of the individual to communicate themselves.

Activists in each station need to explore just what each person's "right to communicate themselves" means in practice. What kind of programming could facilitate this amazing notion? Then, we need to spell out for our community the potential of democratic media as the natural model for those citizens who wish to have a say in how they would like to live in the world. While asking people to support an ideology may be off-putting, we should find little resistance if we ask people and community stations to support human rights, environmental protection and the deepening of democracy at local and global levels. These are issues that stand above all local issues and will constantly impact on the local situation. Any station calling itself a community radio station cannot ignore such issues and their impact on the locality. Shouldn't every community radio station hold the aspiration of alternative media to offer genuine access to its listeners? Surely, some of the local citizens would appreciate such information and value such a communications facility?

Given the scale of problems facing humanity and the failure of current mainstream media to initiate critical dialogue, could we envisage a time when community media would became more prominent, more mainstream, more effective in promoting alternative mindsets and behaviours? We can either acquiesce in global injustice, environmental destruction and economic terrorism, or we can join the struggle, be the voice of civil society in the efforts for justice, democracy and freedom. I believe that such a message has a very large audience waiting to hear it.

3

From Pilot to Policy: The Development of a Community Radio Movement, 1989–1997

Ciarán Kissane

The 1989 to 1997 period was a difficult one for community broadcasters in Ireland. On 31 December 1988, all pirate broadcasters, including a significant number of community broadcasters, had to cease broadcasting if they wanted to be considered for licences under the new regime. The Radio and Television Act 1988 provided a structure for licensing non-RTÉ services for the first time so, from 1 January 1989, the focus shifted from ensuring that the legislative framework accommodated the community sector, to actually securing licences and getting on-air. This was not as straightforward as many expected because there was no real agreement, generally or within the community radio sector itself, about what defined community broadcasting. This question would not be finally resolved until 1997 and this chapter outlines that journey.

The Independent Radio and Television Commission (IRTC, later the Broadcasting Commission of Ireland, BCI) was established under the Radio and Television Act 1988 and was charged with licensing the independent broadcasting sector in Ireland. The 1988 Act specifically mandated the Commission to establish a national independent television station, a national independent radio station and an indefinite number of independent local/community radio services. The Act made no specific distinction between community, commercial or public service-type stations. This openness to different models and approaches to the development of local radio was welcomed by the National Association of Community Broadcasters (NACB) in 1989.

The first IRTC (1989-2003) prioritised the establishment of the national stations (radio and TV) and local county radio services. Twenty-five county licenses were issued in the 1989-1990 period, four of which went to what were, at that point, defined as community radio groups. These were Horizon Radio in North Wicklow, County Sound in North Cork, Tipperary Midwest Radio covering the south and west of Tipperary and Radio Kilkenny covering Kilkenny City and County. In addition, the winning applicants in some of the other areas, such as Kerry, included community radio groups.

As the two Dublin City and County licences had both gone to identifiable commercial radio groups, the community radio lobby in the city continued to press for a further round of licences specifically for community radio stations. However, with the exception of Connemara, there was no significant pressure outside Dublin for additional community radio licensing.

In 1990 the IRTC invited expressions of interest from groups considering providing small-scale community services. However, following the submission of these expressions of interest, no licences were advertised. Among the factors which influenced this decision was the desire to allow the new county services to become established. It is worth noting that in this period the viability of the independent broadcasting sector was under question. This was due to the collapse of the national independent radio station, Century Radio, and to the difficulties being experienced by a number of the new county operators.

In 1991 a temporary licence was issued to a group for a special event station to coincide with Dublin's period as the Cultural Capital of Europe. Following on from this, a single community licence to cover the entire city was advertised in late 1991. This resulted in a split in the NACB in Dublin, between those who supported the idea of a city-wide service and those who favoured a larger number of smaller franchise areas. In the end both of these groups applied for the licence, one group proposing a city-wide service, the other advocating a local opt-out model. The licence was awarded to the former who proposed establishing a public service-type station called Anna Livia Fm. This station is still broadcasting on a city-wide basis as a special interest service. One further community licence was issued by the first IRTC to an Irish language community radio co-operative for the provision of an Irish language station in Dublin and this is Raidió na Life (see Chapter 14). Both Raidió na Life and Anna Livia Fm have been broadcasting in the capital since 1993.

The second IRTC was appointed in autumn 1993 and the new Commission set the further development of community radio as a priority. By this time a number of the community co-operatives who had been awarded county licences had responded to financial pressures by becoming more commercial and in some cases taking on commercial partners. In addition, the independent broadcasting sector had recovered from the shock of the collapse of Century Radio and was finding its feet financially and its voice locally, as the stations attracted significant audience support. However, the fact that there was very little in general programming or operational terms to distinguish county community radio services from local commercial radio services presented a challenge for the Commission. How could it meet the need for additional community licenses without undermining the viability of the local radio sector?

The Commission's response was the initiation of a limited pilot project to see if a model could be developed that would allow for the further development of community radio. Eleven stations were licensed for 18 months and they commenced broadcasting in mid-1995. The pilot group included a mix of city, town and rural stations and those serving geographical communities and communities of interest. The pilot project ran from September 1995 until the end of 1996 with all of the stations receiving a licence extension to allow them remain broadcasting while the IRTC was considering the outcomes. A three-strand evaluation process was adopted for the project which allowed the stations to be evaluated individually, at a group level both by themselves and by the Commission, and at an overall level by the Commission.

A key element of the evaluation structure was the establishment of a Community Radio Forum (the Forum) which would provide an opportunity for stations to meet, discuss issues of common interest and, if possible, to develop joint action plans. In this context, stations were challenged collectively to evaluate progress on an ongoing basis and to develop and implement the required responses. Forum initiatives did not necessarily have to include all of the pilot stations and the Forum was not intended to be the only vehicle for discussion and co-operation.

Six Forum meetings were held during the pilot period and each station was invited to send two representatives to each one. The Forum meetings provided an opportunity for participants to visit other pilot stations and to share practical ideas. This covered programme making, technical issues, fundraising and management. I recall a night in Youghal where a practical demonstration in how to make a studio connection socket using tobacco tins had everyone reassessing the costs of studio construction. While there were obvious differences of opinion amongst participants, the group did gel relatively quickly. A good social element to all Forum meetings contributed to the bonding process. This cohesion was important because within 18 months of being established, the Forum was challenged to develop its own common view of what the outcomes of the pilot project in policy terms should be. The Forum's success in addressing this challenge in many ways laid the foundations for its development since then. Therefore it is worth focusing on the particular event and on those involved in this reflection on the development of community radio during that period.

Following a lengthy discussion at a Forum meeting in Castlebar towards the end of 1996, the task of developing a draft position for discussion by the full group was delegated to a working group. This comprised of Paul Maguire (NEAR Fm), Anne Crowley (Community Radio Castlebar), Tom Murchan (Dublin South Community Radio), Teresa O'Malley (Dublin Weekend Radio) and Sinéad Wylde (Cork Campus Radio). The membership was selected to ensure that different models and experiences were represented at the discussions. The group met in the midlands for convenience, hence it became knows as the "Athlone Group". The meetings were facilitated by Bill Farrell and I attended in an advisory capacity as the IRTC Community Radio Officer.

The group met on a number of occasions over a ten-week period and these discussions allowed station representatives to address the key questions emerging from the pilot project. The pilot project had involved a range of models and not all of these could be accommodated in the future. The "Athlone Group" had to debate what shape future policy should take, bearing in mind that these decisions had real implications for their individual projects. There were lengthy discussions about all of the key issues: ownership and control, staffing, programming and, of course, funding. It was obvious as the work progressed that the emerging consensus had implications for the future of all of the stations, and in particular for Dublin Weekend Radio which was based in Dublin City University. However, to the credit of all those involved, they remained focused on the overall picture rather than on the interests of their own individual stations.

The "Athlone Group" report was less than ten pages in length but it addressed all of the key issues identified by the Forum. It was presented to the Forum at a meeting in the Old Shieling Hotel, Coolock, in March 1997 and, following a lively debate, it was endorsed with some minor modifications by those present. It was submitted to the IRTC as a key information source for its deliberations on the outcomes of the pilot project. The fact that many of the elements in the Forum Report are incorporated in *The IRTC Policy on Community Broadcasting* (1997) is a testimony to the value of the Forum as an evaluation process and a development approach. It is also a testimony to the work of the station representatives who comprised the "Athlone Group" that the sector took the responsibility of developing a viable policy model for the future development of community radio, one which survives largely unchanged today in the BCI's policy on Community Radio Broadcasting (2002) and in the work of the Forum's successor, CRAOL (see Chapter 4).

Following consideration of the lessons emerging from the pilot project, and relevant national and international models and experience, the IRTC finalised its *Policy on Community Radio Broadcasting* in 1997. This relatively short document, which sets out a definition of community radio, was based on a definition developed by the Canadian Radio and Telecommunications Commission in the early 1990s. The Irish version is as follows:

> A community radio station is characterised by its ownership and programming and the community it is authorised to serve. It is owned and controlled by a not-for profit organisation whose structure provides for membership, management, operation and programming primarily by members of the community at large. Its programming should be based on community access and should reflect the special interests and needs of the listenership it is licensed to serve. (IRTC, 1997; BCI, 2002)

The policy recognises the existence of three distinct broadcasting sectors – public, commercial and community. It equally recognises that there is some level of overlap between them. With regard to the community sector, and flowing from the above definition, the document identifies key operational characteristics in relation to ownership, management, funding, programming and the relationship with the community served. It is worth noting that the funding section set down a relatively low minimum viability threshold for community broadcasters – the equivalent of €40,000 per annum.

This recognises that community radio stations are not commercial entities and it is important in ensuring that projects at a relatively early stage of development can secure a licence.

A key development during the pilot period was a recognition by all of the stakeholders that "community" rather than "broadcasting" is the key reference point for the sector. In this context, the wider community sector rather than the broadcasting sector provides applicable models and experiences. This is perhaps best illustrated in the approach that was adopted to audience evaluation. The success of radio, both commercial and public service, is assessed in quantitative listenership terms. It had been argued, even from within the community radio sector, that a similar approach should be adopted for community broadcasting. However such an approach was rejected both by the pilot group through the Forum and by the IRTC. It was agreed that models for evaluating other community development projects rather than broadcasting services were also appropriate for community radio.

In this context an evaluation model, based on a methodology used to evaluate and develop other community action projects, was tested during the pilot period by the Nexus Research Co-operative (Dillon and Ó Siochrú, 1997). The model enabled the community to evaluate its project and allowed those involved in that project to challenge the community to support its continued development and take ownership of their suggested improvements. This approach moved beyond quantitative listenership evaluation and proposed a more qualitative approach to research. It also recognised, in a practical way, that active participation is as important as passive listenership in the context of community radio. The methodology was focused on community feedback workshops, which is an established evaluation methodology in the community sector generally. The workshops considered the community's current impressions of, and relationship with, their station. They explored the potential for developing this relationship and assessed what action plans should be implemented to ensure this relationship is developed. Thus, the community served were not only asked to evaluate the station but also challenged to take responsibility for ensuring development plans were designed and implemented.

In 1998 five-year licences were issued to the nine pilot groups who wished to continue broadcasting as community radio services as now defined. Since then, additional community licences have been awarded in areas where the required level of support has emerged. I think it is fair to say, at this point, that the key factor that has limited the development of additional community broadcasting services in Ireland is the availability of local support and resources, not the licensing regime. In this context the pilot project and the policy which emerged from it can be deemed successful.

4

From a Forum to a Force: The Development of CRAOL, 1998–2007

Nessa McGann

The Community Radio Forum (CRF, or simply "The Forum") was initially set up in 1995 as a result of the work of the then Independent Radio and Television Commission (IRTC, later the Broadcasting Commission of Ireland, BCI), community radio officer Ciarán Kissane (see Chapter 3) and the members of the stations engaged in the pilot project. The Forum began life as a space where community radio practitioners could exchange practical information about running a radio station and formulate a philosophy of community radio in Ireland based on their shared experiences (Day, 2003).

Today the Community Radio Forum represents the 21 licensed community radio stations in Ireland and has registered as a co-operative society which goes by the name of CRAOL, the Irish word for "to broadcast". It administers an annual fund in excess of €120,000, provided by the BCI, and it is recognised as the representative body for community radio by the Irish government and by other national bodies. This chapter is based on a number of interviews with a few key individuals in the life of the Forum/ CRAOL, a comprehensive phone and email survey which I con-

ducted with 17 of the 21 licensed stations, and my own experience as a member of the co-ordinating committee for five years,
including my term as chairperson of CRAOL.

The three main informants were all members of the Executive
Committee of the Forum at various times over these years. Eoin
Brady represented Wired FM, the Limerick-based student station.
Brady is now a producer with RTÉ Lyric in Limerick. Declan
McLoughlinn was the station manager of Tallaght Community Radio (TCR) in Dublin. McLoughlin is now the Licensing and Com-
pliance Officer with the BCI. Niamh Farren was the station manager of Radio Corca Baiscinn in Co. Clare. Farren is now the Outreach Co-ordinator with the Media Co-op/NEAR Fm in Dublin.

By 1998, nine stations had successfully completed the pilot project phase for community radio and were fully licensed. Three of
these were campus stations based in third-level institutions (Cork
Campus Radio, based in UCC, FLIRT Fm, based in UCG (now NUI
Galway) and the then Galway RTC and Wired Fm, based in Mary
Immaculate College, the Limerick Institute of Technology and the
University of Limerick). There were three stations based in the
capital, Dublin (DSCR, in the south of the city, NEAR, in the north
east and WDCR in West Dublin). There were also three rural stations (CRY, based around the town of Youghal, Co. Cork, CRC,
based around the town of Castlebar, Co. Mayo and CCR, based in
Letterfrack, North Connemara Co. Galway).

In 1998, the Community Radio Forum organised itself so that
each licensed community radio station would nominate two representatives to attend meetings of the Community Radio Forum
which were held every six months. The individual representatives
could change from meeting to meeting but the idea was to ensure
fair representation from all stations and to try to maintain a balance between paid members of staff and volunteers. From the stations' representatives, four members were elected from four different stations to sit on a co-ordinating committee. This was the
main working group of the Forum and met on a more frequent

basis than the general Forum, on average once every two months. A chairperson, secretary, treasurer and vice-chairperson were elected from within this group. While working groups were set up during this period (1998-1999), these were on an ad-hoc basis and met as such (Brady).

While the Community Radio Forum had already achieved the task of formulating a policy on community radio, adopted by the then IRTC and still in use today (IRTC, 1997; BCI, 2002, see Chapter 3), it was at this time, 1998, still unsure of its own role and how to achieve its aspirations, as an organisational body for community radio. Brady remembers that during this period the Forum was trying to articulate who they were as a group and re-members references to Canada and Europe and how practitioners in those countries were making community radio. He says that the CRF talked about what Ireland should be doing and this in-cluded starting a programme exchange system and organising in-formation sessions on funding and training (Brady; Day, 2003). However, he notes that while many things were discussed, many times during many general Forum meetings, no decisions were arrived at and no action was taken.

At this time, stations had only been on air for three years and many working within the sector were still new to the practicali-ties of running a community radio station. Brady comments that:

> We [the Forum] were caught between having paid radio staff not having the time to look above the parapet of their own bailiwick and volunteers in the Forum who had time but didn't have the same expertise to put into training or into some of the other ideas that were being discussed.

McLoughlinn echoes this feeling of people being too busy to take on the extra responsibility of running a national organisation:

> It was still a very new organisation in 2000 and it's a lot more professional now ... I think that most of the effort up to 1997 was on the policy document and getting everything estab-

lished really. At that stage most people were far too busy in
their own stations, never mind developing the sector.

As a result of the heavy workloads of individuals within their
stations and the ability of the Forum to endlessly discuss issues
without making much visible progress, both Brady and McLoughlinn comment that during 1998-2000 the Forum was regarded as a
talking shop by many of its members. The apparent lack of relevance or the absence of practical support to the majority of the
stations at this time left the Forum "slightly in limbo" (Farren).

By 2000, both McLoughlinn and Farren were on the co-
ordinating committee of the CRF and realised that the organisation needed to consider its future direction. A day-long evaluation
was organised to examine the strengths and weaknesses of the
organisation and the ambitions which community radio stations
had for it. A year-long plan was initiated as a result of this day and
people were nominated to carry out certain tasks and responsi-
bilities. McLoughlinn noted that "this overall refocus certainly
worked, you can see it in how the Forum has developed since
then, how effective it is".

Since 1995 the Forum had always been funded by the IRTC to
hold meetings where the cost of the meeting room, lunch and a
stipend towards travel costs would be met through the Community Radio Support Scheme (CRSS), a fund applied for by the Forum and administered by the IRTC. In 2000 the co-ordinating
committee decided to apply for a new round of the community
support scheme which would include two ventures designed to
address key concerns of its members. The first of these became
the Community Radio Training Féile festival, which is discussed
later in the context of training, the second was ethos promotion,
which is described in the discussion of the future of CRAOL.

The renewed sense of vigour brought to the Community Radio Forum by this committee led to a number of important developments in the organisation and in the day-to-day organisation

of the committee. Firstly, they identified the need for members in stations (not sitting at the general Forum level or as members of the co-ordinating committee) to become involved in working groups in order to promote ownership of the Forum by the member stations. Secondly, they prioritised certain areas, such as training and ethos promotion, to demonstrate the value of belonging to such a network to the general members. Thirdly, they implemented a more cohesive communications strategy – between the members of the sub groups, the executive committee and the general Forum. The movement away from a talking shop to becoming a dynamic network had begun in earnest.

From 2001 to 2006 I was involved with the network as a member of the co-ordinating committee and I experienced the influence that the working groups have had on the productivity of the Forum. Spreading the work around has ensured that the stations themselves contribute to the work of the Forum and this has brought the benefits of improved information circulation and more active ownership of the organisation. I first became involved with the Forum as part of the first Training Féile subgroup, and through my participation I began to understand the ability of this organisation to really impact on the sector.

During 2001–2003 the co-ordinating committee began to meet more frequently and issues around the promotion of the sector to its members and the general public began to be addressed. The idea of a website was mooted, addressing the "What is community radio?" question, often asked by funders, by government agencies, by other actors on the broadcast landscape and indeed by members of the Forum itself. Developing a national identity has been important to the Forum since 1995 and remains relevant today. To date, community radio has not been as successful as it needs to be in promoting awareness of its ethos of community empowerment through participation in the medium of radio.

In 2002 the co-ordinating committee advertised a process of tendering for independent research on the link between community radio and community development. This resulted in the published research *Community Radio in Ireland: Its Contribution to Community Development* (Unique Perspectives, 2003), which clearly demonstrated the close link between this kind of radio and the community development work undertaken in Ireland. Publishing this research was very important at this time for the Forum. The co-ordinating committee and invited members of the Forum had just succeeded in finally meeting the Minister for Communications, Dermot Aherne, TD. Farren notes that this meeting was continually postponed by the Department and the resultant ten minute meeting was very frustrating for the committee. This meeting was held in early 2003 to argue the case for a legislative definition of community radio and in order to ring-fence funding for the sector, from the forthcoming Public Service Broadcast Fund (Now the BCI's Sound and Vision Scheme). While the meeting itself might not have yielded results on those issues, it did name and present the united face for community radio to the Department of Communications, which has led to an increase of acknowledgment from the department for the organisation, as the representative body for the sector.

The research that had been commissioned at a Forum meeting in early 2003 indicated that the Community Radio Forum of Ireland needed to revamp its own organisational identity. A new name was chosen, CRAOL, and it was agreed that a new identity with a logo, a website and a strategy for self-promotion should be developed. In the Forum meeting later that year, the general members agreed on the current logo and also agreed to start a quarterly newsletter for distribution amongst stations, donors and other community organisations.

In addition to promoting itself and the ethos of community radio, the Forum began to organise a number of additional initiatives to give practical assistance to Forum members in terms of training and funding in 2003-04 (McLoughlinn). These initiatives inspired a number of very positive general meetings of the Forum. High attendance and a return to the fold of a few stations which had distanced themselves from the work of the Forum over the years indicate clearly that the new structures are working.

During 2003/2004 the Forum began to seriously talk about the need to become a legal entity. Initially constituted as a loose network of community radio stations, it had become obvious that the next step was to organise formally. This would open up possibilities for the network, especially in terms of securing funding for CRAOL and the possible employment of a national co-ordinator. A subgroup dedicated to investigating various legal options open to the Forum came to the opinion that the structure of a co-operative society would be best in keeping with the movement and the Forum agreed. Over a period of 18 months, articles of association were drawn up ensuring that CRAOL would continue to function as a democratic and accountable organisation for its members while remaining true to the ideals of the AMARC Europe Charter (see appendix). In April 2005, the first AGM was held in Dublin. Those involved were optimistic:

> I think that the whole incorporation thing is a real achievement for the organisation and it may lead the network in a new direction. Hopefully it will provide a strong platform for community stations, but it will also learn from the experience of other networks and doesn't stop being relevant for the grass roots members (Farren).

However, the need to do more, to continue to develop into the future was also recognised:

> CRAOL could certainly do with a full time employee, that was discussed in my time and even before that – the development of the CRF in the co-op is a good idea and should help on that (McLoughlinn).

So, what does CRAOL actually do? As well as lobbying on behalf of the sector, the Community Radio Forum had always acted
as a space for sharing experiences and advice between individual
member stations and the practitioners involved. This was recognised as one of its greatest strengths and throughout its existence
this directly informed the practical work-plans of the Forum "We
have strength in numbers and in the early days we needed to protect ourselves" (Brady). McLoughlinn says:

> You see how important the Forum is on a national level when
> you go to a Féile meeting, that's a two day encapsulation of
> what community radio can offer – support from stations, net-
> working, affirmation of what you are doing. Sometimes differ-
> ent stations will be having varying degrees of an easy time, a
> station might have a very good run of it, great funding and
> good people working there and then five or six years later
> they are having difficulty paying the electricity bill.

And Farren agrees:

> I learnt a lot from the cups of coffee and pints I drank with
> the other managers and board members, some of whom gave
> me great support when things weren't going so well for my
> own station. Meeting people at Forum meetings made it so
> much easier to pick up the phone when you had a problem.

On a day-to-day level CRAOL engages in many areas of work.
These include lobbying on behalf of the sector to government
agencies, to the BCI, to national agencies, to funders and to others. CRAOL submits a proposal for a funding scheme (the Community Radio Support Scheme, CRSS) to the BCI on an annual
basis and liaises with its officers to plan training. It organises training and development workshops for its members and it gives advice and support to community organisations (which it terms "aspirant stations"), when they are in the process of applying for
community radio licences. It promotes the ethos of community

radio both nationally and to its own members. Farren is proud of the fact that:

> It provides a unified voice for the sector which is so much more powerful and effective when it comes to influencing policy … it has the potential to be a great source of support for newer and developing stations, and, at international level, it provides the infrastructure to contribute to a global network.

All of the work of CRAOL is laid out in the Community Radio Support Scheme (CRSS). This budget is compiled and costed by members of the co-ordinating committee and agreed by the general Forum before it is submitted through the Training and Development officer of the BCI for the approval of the Commission. The budget has grown year on year with a budget approved at €60,000 for six months in 2005 during my last term of office. The scheme usually funds four main areas – networking, ethos promotion, evaluation and training – and each of these is of value.

Networking costs cover all meetings of sub-groups, the Executive (previously the co-ordinating committee) and the general Forum meetings. Costs include travel expenses for participants (possible facilitation costs), refreshments (usually lunch) and room hire. Ethos promotion has covered a number of areas in recent years, from the commissioning of independent research on the sector to publishing and distributing a CRAOL newsletter, free pens and t-shirts for members, to training in website development and maintenance (see www.craol.ie). A management handbook is being compiled, a community radio roadshow has been developed to travel to the parts of the country which have yet to experience the joys of owning their own community radio station, and plans are afoot to host an annual community radio awards event which would be based on principles other than competition. All of these initiatives will help to promote the community radio movement in the public consciousness. This book itself is part of that initiative to heighten awareness and understanding of the potential value of community radio stations to communities all over Ireland and maybe further afield.

Evaluation is the only part of the budget currently not administered by the Treasurer of CRAOL and it is the second largest strand of the budget. Standing at €21,000 in 2005-2006, it is seen as extremely important for the future development of the community radio sector. It is administered by a sub-group comprised of a member of CRAOL's Executive, a member of a recognised community development group, and two executive officers of the BCI (see Chapter 11). Under the internal evaluation strand of the scheme, stations may apply for funding to conduct a wide range of activities. These include the consultative process required in preparing a mission statement, devising a training plan for the station or drawing up a volunteer charter. This fund is specifically aimed at building the organisational capacity of the individual station itself and is open to all licensed community radio stations. The external fund is also open to all licensed stations who may apply to evaluate their relationship with their audience and community. Some stations may seek listenership figures; for example, Connemara Community Radio used their grant to pay for an independent MRBI poll of listeners in 2001. Others may conduct more qualitative studies around community participation in their stations, for example the NEAR-NEXUS Report of 2003.

Training remains the most important and visible part of the work of CRAOL and the Community Radio Training Féile is the biggest activity organised annually. First held in 2001, in Kilkee, Co. Clare, the original idea to apply for funding and to hold the Féile came from the co-ordinating committee of 2000 (Farren; McLoughlinn; see Chapter 11). Each year member stations apply to host the Féile and the station chosen works with a sub-group made up of a representative of the BCI (usually the Training and Development Officer), a representative from the previous year's host station and a member of the co-ordinating committee.

Farren worked very closely on the first application to the BCI to fund this new venture as there was no budget allocated to such an initiative under the CRSS at the time. As station manager of Radio Corca Baiscinn, she was also part of the first station to hold this event and her leadership in both areas was outstanding. Radio Corca Baiscinn is based in the small seaside town of Kilkee on the west coast of Clare and the station had only received its licence in 1999. Nearly 100 people – paid workers, volunteers and board members – attended and all of the 15 stations licensed at the time were represented. She recalls the event:

> I'll never forget the feeling of a hundred community radio activists descending on a small seaside resort for the week, and the buzz of really being part of something. Even though the facilities weren't ideal, you were left struck by the desire of people to exchange ideas and talk about what they were doing in their own stations. And, for our community, it did a lot in terms of PR for our station.

The Féile is run over a weekend, chosen by the host station. Friday nights are introductory and mainly social. The bulk of the formal training is conducted on Saturday, from early morning until somewhere around 6.00 pm. On Saturday evening there is a general conference dinner followed by some serious socialising. Sunday morning either takes the form of discussion meetings or the live broadcast of a debate, but each station chosen to host the Féile has the opportunity to guide the general structure of the event.

The 2001 Féile was an extremely well run and positive time for all who took part. Its success was gauged by the fact that so many people had attended and that all stations, informally and formally, endorsed the principle that practitioners in community radio in Ireland needed a space to meet each other, share ideas and advice and learn new skills.

As a result of this, the Training Féile has been incorporated into the annual CRSS budget and is perhaps one of the most important parts of the workplan for each Executive Committee of CRAOL. The importance of the Féile to the sector has also been realised by the BCI, whose executive officers have attended all the Féilte, either to take part or to facilitate particular workshops. Members of the Commission of the BCI have also attended the Féile, and the Commission recognises the importance of the Féile concretely by providing increased budgetary supports for this annual event in each CRSS since 2001.

The actual training element of the Féile is designed to give participants a taste of or an introduction to the various skills needed to work in community broadcasting. Saturday is taken up with a selection of themed strands of workshops running concurrently. Well in advance of the Féile, each station is asked to specify the workshops or areas in which it feels its participants need training. These are then collated and a number of strands, usually five or six, are constructed. Workshops have been offered in technical and programme production skills, PC-based editing, broadcasting and law, evaluating the policies and processes of a community radio station, running board meetings, documentary making, news and current affairs in community radio, including children in community radio broadcasting, broadcasting on the web, the ethos of community radio and many other diverse topics.

The workshops concentrate on offering practical skills to practitioners. There are also discussion sessions on various aspects of the community radio project, which include reflections on the ethos of community radio, analysis of the role of women in community radio, plans for delivering development education through community radio and constant re-evaluation of the aims and practices of community radio in Ireland. Most of the trainers are now sourced from within the community radio sector, which is a good indication of how much the sector has progressed and matured since 1994. Representatives from national community development organisations are also invited in order to inject fresh ideas into the movement, for community radio activists to learn from the experience of others and for those groups to meet community radio broadcasters face to face. All workshops and the trainers or facilitators who run them are evaluated by a number of different parties. All those who participate in the workshops report on each session, as does the station hosting the Féile and the sub-group which is responsible to CRAOL for hosting the Féile. A final report is submitted to CRAOL and this outlines the budget and evaluates the entire event and is used in guiding the processes and policies of the next year's Féile.

Féilte are very exciting events in their own right. They provide a chance for people who live far apart, all over the country, to come together and to celebrate the ethos and achievements of community radio. While many staff and station managers of radio stations meet throughout the year at the CRAOL Forum and Executive and at sub-group meetings, volunteers who contribute to their own station rarely have the chance to meet other volunteers and to build relationships. Broadening out the training offered and building a space where all stations are invited to participate re-emphasises the ownership of CRAOL by its member stations and by the individual practitioners within them. The importance of providing workshops for programme makers, station managers and other staff, as well as for members of the board of directors of stations, has always been emphasised. According to McLoughlinn, "The Féile needs to offer something for everyone involved in community radio".

In a bid to answer the call from stations on the need for accredited training in community radio, the Forum registered as a national centre with the Further Education and Training Accreditation Council (FETAC) in 2002. Accredited training is important in terms of the personal development of participants, both paid staff and volunteers. It provides stations with a source of income (from national and local training bodies) and recognisably builds the overall capacity of the sector. However, up to 2004 there were no specific community radio accredited courses available from any nationally recognised training organisation or body. CRAOL developed two separate training modules at levels 1 and 2 with FETAC. A day-long information session was held in Galway in late 2004 which informed stations about the process of entering candidates for this national accreditation. It laid out the syllabus (developed by the CRF in 2003) and the marking system (developed by the CRF in 2004). While the training modules are delivered in-house by the stations themselves, they are co-ordinated and administered by a single nominated station. It is this station that submits the paperwork to the national accredited body.

The first series of these courses was delivered in two stations in 2005 and all participants achieved a high standard. A further six stations submitted participants for the courses in 2006 and demand continues to grow. CRAOL expects that any individual working in community radio will soon be able to avail of these courses.

As a result of the increased workshops offered at each successive Féile and the increase in the amount of training being offered by CRAOL through the FETAC scheme, the co-ordinating committee of 2003/2004 recognised the need to accredit practitioners from within the community radio movement itself to serve the sector. There was a recognition of the huge wealth of experience that exists within the sector and a recognition that training community radio activists to train others in the movement would benefit both CRAOL and the individuals who possessed this practical experience. It was also deemed necessary in order to respond to increasing calls from aspirant community radio stations requesting trainers with practical community radio experience. CRAOL has now run two courses of training for trainers, accredited by a nationally-recognised accreditation body, the Irish Institute of Training and Development (IITD). As a result of this process there are now 22 accredited trainers and more courses are planned. This process was organised by Áine Lyne, secretary to CRAOL and former station manager of FLIRT in Galway, with the support of Stephanie Comey during her time as Training and Development Officer of the BCI.

Formulating a response to the challenges of answering the "what is community radio" question to individuals and aspirant stations has led to an interest in providing an e-learning solution. This project, the brainchild of Jack Byrne of NEAR Fm, is currently underway and it is hoped that this service will be available through the CRAOL website, www.craol.ie.

The relationship between the regulator (the BCI) and the regulated (Irish community radio stations) has been critical in terms of the overall development of the sector. In the early days (1994-1999) community radio, while seen as a minority presence in terms of its position within the broadcasting landscape, had an official link to the then IRTC (now the BCI) through a dedicated Community Radio Development Officer, Ciarán Kissane. Day notes that community radio in Ireland was fortunate that Mr. Kissane was both well-informed about, and well-intentioned towards, community radio worldwide (Day, 2003). The initial role played by Kissane as a facilitator rather than as an inspector indicated to the Forum that he was a supporter of community radio (Brady; Day, 2003). This initial relationship has been developed and deepened by each of the subsequent executive officers of the BCI with responsibility for Training and Development. Unfortunately, the role of Community Radio Development Officer has been discontinued and the Training and Development Officer now works with both commercial and community radio and television stations and their representative organisations. While the people appointed to this office continued to be positively supportive of community radio, their focus has been, inevitably, split.

The Training and Development Officer of the BCI attends the general meetings of CRAOL, in a supportive capacity, and also sits on a number of sub-groups such as the Féile sub-group. The opportunity to pick up the phone and to receive the benefit of great organisational experience, friendly advice, the willingness and openness to discuss new issues, problems and projects with successive officers (Stephanie Comey, Ita Kenneally and Margaret Tumelty) is a clear indication of the kind of support offered by the BCI to ensure the positive development of CRAOL. Farren's perception of the relationship between the BCI and CRAOL is that the regulator:

> had very much a supportive and facilitative role during the whole process of CRAOL's development. I know that the BCI has bought into the whole idea of "strategic networking" with the aim of strengthening national networks so that they can begin to address their own needs, and this has worked well in terms of the freedom that we had to organise the Féile.

The future of CRAOL lies in its continued relevance to the member stations and in its ability to articulate the views and concerns of the community radio movement in Ireland. We cannot rest now on self-congratulations. We need to keep our focus on the reason for our existence: the promotion and development of the ethos of community radio and the support of a shared network for licensed and aspirant stations in terms of training and all other developments.

The broadcasting landscape in Ireland may significantly change with the introduction of new legislation. CRAOL must seize such opportunities to demand our right to be clearly legislated for and represented on any new body which regulates the industry. We need to clearly articulate the views of our stations to the government and to those who wish to write us off as "merely the third sector". CRAOL must continue to rise to the challenge of providing relevant training opportunities for volunteers, paid staff and board members in the licensed stations. We must ensure that the force which we have forged from the Forum continues to pursue our joint aims of ethos promotion and network facilitation so that CRAOL supports and develops the community radio movement in Ireland.

PART TWO

Aims and Issues

5

Community Radio and
Community Development

Rosemary Day

Media do not create community but they can help to build it. Community radio activists see radio as a useful tool in achieving their aim of improving the society and community in which they live. The emphasis on participation, on non-hierarchical ways of working, on self-management and on process rather than on goal achievement bears a strong resemblance to the established professional discipline of community development. Community radios, in their aims and organisation, are similar to the community development projects pioneered by Saul Alinsky in the US in the 1950s. They owe a great deal to development practices in the third world, for example the liberation theology of Paulo Freire in Latin America from the 1970s and the participative communication practices of the 1980s and 1990s in much of the developing world. They have also learned from the community development projects sponsored by governments in Western Europe and elsewhere since the 1980s. Voluntary organisations in Ireland are moving away from the status of charities run by religious orders, as they were in the nineteenth and twentieth centuries, to community-development style projects in the twenty-first century.

However, while the community radio project seeks to develop the community, this is not exactly what "community development" as a term means. "Community development" describes particular work practices which, in Ireland, are usually undertaken by paid professionals. As a general term, it describes ways of working with groups to develop the community and to empower those who are marginalised, particularly by poverty, racism and sexism, to help themselves. "Community development" and "developing the community" are complimentary goals but they are not synonymous. The development of community is broader and describes an ideal rather than a particular practice. Community development is a practice and is far more narrowly focused than the ideal of the development of a community. Community development has evolved as a clearly defined way of carrying out social and community work and as a recognised discipline within academia.

Professional community workers in Ireland see community development as a powerful tool for engineering social change from the personal, through the communal and on to the political level. The Community Action Network (CAN) in Ireland describes this process as follows:

> Community Development aims to encourage people to take control of their lives, to develop fully their human potential and to promote community empowerment. It involves people coming together in groups to identify their collective needs and to develop programmes to meet these needs. The process or the way the work is carried out is as important as the programme of development being undertaken. The process of Community Development stresses the need to develop community awareness, engender group cohesiveness, and promote self reliance and collective action. This logically leads communities to seek change at policy and institutional levels, often highlighting the need for the redistribution of society's resources (Kelleher and Whelan, 1992).

The social goals of improving the quality of life and of reducing the levels of social inequities may be, but are not necessarily, part of the remit of Irish community radio stations. However, the lofty goals of developing greater understanding in support of peace, tolerance, democracy and development are dear to community radio activists and are specifically mentioned in point 10 of the AMARC Europe Charter, which states that:

> Community radio seeks to foster exchange between community radio broadcasters using communications to develop greater understanding in support of peace, tolerance, democracy and development. (See appendix).

Community radio activists share many of the same aims as practitioners of community development but they define a wider role for themselves in society. In many instances community radio can assist community development work as a channel of communication. Point 1 of the AMARC Europe Charter states that community radio specifically aims to:

> promote the right to communicate, assist the free flow of information, to encourage creative expression and to contribute to the democratic process and to enable the development of a pluralist society. (See appendix).

Community development supports and attempts to enable the democratisation of society at all levels but does not make communication a priority as community radio, almost by definition, must do.

Community development is frequently the mode of practice used by community radio stations to organise their work. Community radio aims to work in a participative and democratic manner. The projects are owned and managed by the community on a not-for-profit basis. Stress is laid on the process more than on the achievement of goals. The empowerment of individuals and of communities is of primary importance. In summary, it is fair to say that community radio can use community development as a work practice, as a useful tool, while encompassing many, but not all, of its aims.

Community radio stations can and do define the communities with which they work. In many cases these mirror the communities targeted by community development work, such as marginalised and disadvantaged minorities. In others, the community served may encompass a wider range of socio-economic groupings and come closer to the remit of a public service broadcasting station. The definition of the community, or of groups within a community, which a station chooses to target will influence its work practices and organisation and will have implications in relation to sources of funding, for programming choices and for station ethos. Community development workers in Ireland are inclined to stress the importance of working with the dis-empowered, the voiceless and the disenfranchised and seek to effect these changes through the grassroots or "bottom up" approach. Community development in Ireland has come to be very narrowly focused on working with those who are marginalised by society especially through poverty, racism and sexism, as the Area Development Management project (ADM) in Ireland describes it as follows:

> Community Development is about enabling people to enhance their capacity to play a role in shaping the society of which they are a part. It works towards helping groups and communities to articulate needs and viewpoints and to influence the processes that structure their everyday lives. It is recognised that the ability to participate fully in society is open more to some groups and individuals than others, therefore the priority for those engaged in integrated local social and economic development is to work with the most disadvantaged (ADM, 1999).

This is both admirable and radical but a cynic will note that funds are available to work with those most marginalised in society, for example Travellers, the long-term unemployed and, more recently, new immigrants. Of course community radio stations should prioritise such groups but they need to assess the risk of pursuing funding which enables them to work with certain target groups in the community and may cause them to forget their remit to all members of the community which they serve. Government interventions via community development projects to alleviate the effects of poverty in rural and urban Ireland do not aim to build all sectors of the community equally. Self-organised community groups which seek to build a strong sense of community, to create a public sphere in which all members can participate and to improve the quality of life for all, have a wider and potentially more radical role to play than such government-funded initiatives.

Community development by paid professionals is a vital and important way of developing community, but it is not the only way. The current focus by state-sponsored community development workers in Ireland may not be helpful to community development long term, to communities in general or to community radio in particular. By concentrating on those who are marginalised in isolation from the community as a whole, they risk institutionalising their marginalisation. All community development projects need to bring all sectors of the community along together if real change is to occur in attitudes and values, as well as in material conditions. Funding agencies and community development workers are aware of the need for the integration of marginalised people into mainstream society but they need to work with the greater community also for this to happen. Those who are not considered to be marginalised also need to be educated and to be persuaded of the benefits of working collaboratively, equitably and inclusively and community radio projects are ideally suited to this work.

Many community radio activists do not view their role as being exclusively that of working with the powerless or the disenfranchised. Many Irish community stations operate in middle class or mixed socio-economic areas and they see their role as serving all of the members of those communities. This may include a special remit for the less advantaged members of the community as is the case in West Dublin Area Radio (WDAR, originally West Dublin Community Radio, WDCR), or it may not. Some community radios broadcast in the most affluent communities of Ireland, for example DSCR, in South County Dublin. In these cases, and in rural stations with a mixed socio-economic demography, it would be dangerous and unhelpful to concentrate solely on the disempowered, ignoring the talents and needs of the better educated, wealthier and more privileged members of those communities. Community radio seeks to connect the entire community to itself and to enrich the entire community as a whole, not just parts of it, although it may employ community development tactics to do this. The divisions of class, gender, religion, ethnicity and language are all important considerations, but truly inclusive community building will seek to accommodate all and to build bridges across these divides within communities.

The type of social capital which community radio stations try to build will reveal the priorities for each individual station. Does it attempt to bond members of that community closer together or to build bridges between diverse elements of the community or, ideally, does it attempt to do both? The philosophical orientation of the community radio movement in relation to building community can be identified, in part, by an examination of the benefits which Irish community radio stations hope will accrue to their communities by virtue of the participation of members of their communities in their ownership, management and programming.

Community media have been recognised as useful tools for community development. Several of the community radio stations currently licensed in Ireland were set up initially by "parent" community development organisations. These include Raidió Pobail Inis Eoghain, set up by Inishowen Rural Development Ltd in Donegal; Raidió Corca Baiscinn, set up by Éirí Corca Baiscinn in Clare; and Connemara Community Radio (CCR), set up partly by ConWest Plc in Galway. In these areas, where community development is strongly established, the stations are seen as an ideal way of providing information and education to widely dispersed populations. They are seen as providing a communications link for the community and of presenting the community to itself in a positive light. They are also seen as sites for training in basic skills, as a way of enabling people to return to the job market through community employment (CE) schemes, and as a vehicle for increasing the self-confidence of individuals and therefore their ability to become actors in the life of their own communities. It seems a logical step for all community development activists to investigate the potential community radio offers to their own projects. The community radio station provides a communications link and another way of networking and of empowering people through participation.

The remainder of this chapter is based on research which I conducted for a Ph.D thesis (Day, 2003). I continued to research the work of Irish community radio stations and those findings are available in my recently published book (Day, 2007). However, the insights offered by the people who are quoted here have not been published before. I am grateful to the respondents who are named here and to many others active in Irish community radio for sharing their time and reflections with me.

The aim of building the community which they serve is the primary aim for all community radio stations. The ways they set about doing this and the priorities they place on different objectives vary across stations, but many Irish community radio stations today employ community development practices to powerful effect. WDAR revised the whole thrust of their operation in response to the needs of their community. Unlike most community radio stations in Ireland which grew from grassroots demands for licences, WDAR grew originally from a college's need to provide practical work for its media students. They only got to know the community which they served when they started to work with them. Their aims changed fundamentally when the station staff recognised the realities and the needs of the community they were serving and began to respond to them. This is expressed in their early mission statement:

> By providing access for the community to a service of information, education and entertainment, West Dublin Community Radio seeks to act as an impetus for the stimulation of community activity, identity and well-being (WDCR, 1994).

Chairperson Celia Flanagan explains their change of direction in community development terms:

> That type of deep community development, that people use it as a tool and that the idea for the use can come from anywhere. It sometimes comes from us because sometimes I think you have to prod the community, you see things that can be done and sometimes I think you have to have a leadership role. Then again, if someone comes to you and they're very confident about what they're doing or what ever, you can give them the leadership role, depending on the circumstance.

Station staff at WDAR are keenly aware of the potential their station has to develop the whole person. This is carried through in the personal relationship which they nurture with each volunteer, Community Employment (CE) Scheme worker, board member or casual visitor to the studios. They believe in working co-operatively, non-hierarchically and in assisting people in finding their own voices. Former station manager Eugene Bollard explains one of the important effects which the foundation of the radio has had as follows:

> In this area very few go on to third level, the radio has made the college accessible to them – they can walk in. Their own confidence, their own speech, it gives more options to them and I think that's a huge thing.

Bollard himself is a good example of this. He started with the station as a participant in the CE scheme and became the station manager while studying for a degree at night. Without using the rhetoric of community development, staff at WDAR are concerned about facilitating the participation of those most marginalised by society and of working in a non-hierarchical and empowering way. Celia Flanagan explains that this is what makes their working day worthwhile:

> I get a great buzz out of watching someone come on, people who mightn't say a word for the first three months and then they do every thing on the one day – talk, write, go on air.

The goal and the ethos of community development were the founding principles of Connemara Community Radio (CCR). These principles and aims were clarified over the first four years of the station's existence and their second application for a licence in 1998 rephrases them as follows:

> The aim of Connemara Community Radio is to operate a community radio station that adheres to the principles of good community practice, i.e widespread participation, empowerment, ready access by all especially the most marginalised. We are firmly located in the community development tradition and see radio as a highly significant and appropriate vehicle in this process (CCR, 1998).

They elaborate on this and state their aims clearly and concretely as being:

- To establish a community radio service in the context of being aware of the potential of radio to enhance the process of community development in novel and innovative ways

- A commitment to the establishment of a radio service which is truly community owned, managed and operated

- A commitment to the development of a service which acknowledges the complexity and diversity of communities and of different interests within them (CCR, 1998).

These aims were formulated through a process of self-evaluation and discussion at volunteer meetings and workshops, an essential part of any community development project. Each volunteer and worker believes in the community development goals and principles of the station and is proud that this is what they are about. Their first station manager, Mary Ruddy, clarifies their position:

> I think really what I would say about community radio is that it's a tool for community development but obviously it's a specific one. It's a broadcasting one, so a lot of your concerns will be as they are with the commercial and the public ones, you know programming, problems with programming, transmission problems, technologies. So we will share these things with broadcasters, but the other end of it, you know, "the why we're there", the kind of more philosophical end of it, is more comfortably located in the community and voluntary field.

This is held to be true by everyone participating in the station. People in CCR tend to describe their community in a block and then as specific subgroups. Some of these subgroups are to the forefront in programming provision, such as the community of local artists and local community activists. Others, more marginalised, are targeted by the station and become empowered through training and participation, such as women in the home and young people who have left school early.

NEAR Fm sees itself as bringing the various groups in the community together and enhancing their own development work through their involvement with the station and each other. The former chairperson, Jack Byrne, reflects:

> So a lot of these things link in together. I think what, for me, the richness of community radio is that it can actually allow people with compatible but slightly different approaches to this issue of development to use the radio station to pursue

their own particular developmental aims and I think they're all complimentary. I don't see a conflict in that.

The understanding of community development itself and of the role which radio could play in enabling this practice was not fully understood at first, but it grew and evolved as the founding group experimented and interacted with other community radio activists from around the world. As Jack Byrne explains:

> I think there was an instinctive grasp that media and radio could be good for community development, now it was as nebulous as that. It was like one of these things, you ran it up the flag pole and everybody saluted it and no one quite knew what it meant. What did we mean by access and participation and that sort of thing?

NEAR Fm also takes its role as an educator very seriously. It works to educate the community in a number of ways, as an information source certainly, but also by equipping people with the skills, both radio-specific and personal development, to hear their own voices, to articulate their problems and to find the solutions to them.

Examples of this aim being translated into practice include the work they do with refugees, prisoner rehabilitation, early school leavers and Travellers (see Chapter 6). Not all of these have been successful but the station manager explained that people in NEAR Fm understand the slow nature of community development work and do not view a high drop-out rate or the collapse of a project as outright failure. This is common in community development projects where the emphasis is placed on the process rather than on the product, on working at the level with which people can cope.

The goal of empowering the disadvantaged and of being an instrument in enabling people to change their own environment and circumstances is very strong in this station. Jack Byrne is passionate about the role he believes NEAR Fm can play in this way:

It's community development but for me, for me I think it is about personal empowerment. I really would love to think that the station was empowering people, that just to help them, just to help people to realise their own uniqueness and their own potential. I'm sort of getting in to something maybe even more spiritual than that, I would love to think that people understood their own ability to change things, that in the sort of world of chaos each person can have an impact, each person can have an impact on the situation, if they just realise their power to organise. Then of course, I feel you need to be informed, to organise, to do certain things, rather than always sort of acting to other people's agendas, that they start writing their own agendas and for me, that's when I think the station will have arrived and I don't see that happening in the next twelve months even. I'd love to be at the stage where the station, through its programming, was making people aware of this power that they have and to question, not to be complacent, I mean, for me, we should be asking what is an economy for? Is it just about the Celtic Tiger or is it about the weakest and the poorest and ensuring that they have a say in the whole thing?

Every Irish community radio station recognises the power of community radio to build their community. They are all concerned that community activists locally use their stations to accomplish their own goals. In reflecting on the development of Connemara Community Radio (CCR) in its first five years as a licensed broadcaster, their first station manager, Mary Ruddy, believes that people gradually came to realise the benefits of community radio in advertising or promoting their own group's activities. The situation has changed dramatically from the early days when it was difficult for other groups to visualise the benefits of participating in the station. Today, groups and associations are keen to go on air in order to have an impact on the community at large. They believe that the community radio station is a good way to promote themselves and their activities. As Mary Ruddy explains:

I think people do use the station as a tool and increasingly so. I think there was a time, initially, when we started doing commentaries for example, we found the GAA impossible to depend on. Now they come to us and they will sort out where we will get access to a telephone line, they'll look for sponsors... And I think, certainly it raises awareness of what the groups are doing. Yacht clubs, for example, the RNLI would frequently have made contact with us about say a new development, a new boat, how many rescues they had, how many call outs they had and I think it just makes people aware of "God, I wouldn't have thought the Clifden RNLI would be that active" or so on. I think as well that one of the things that it generally does is to make people aware of the level of activity in the area.

NEAR Fm believe that they have succeeded in making their station available to community groups to broadcast their message to the community and that these groups recognise the value of the station to them in doing so. Station personnel quote several examples of groups who have experienced the positive benefits of going on air with NEAR Fm (see Chapter 6) and of groups who consequently became closely involved with the station. They are convinced that the access they can offer groups is more meaningful than that offered by other media because it is continuous, as Jack Byrne explains:

I think community radio's real strength is that it allows individuals and organisations this continuous access to keep telling their story and as it evolves, to tell people where they're at now and to bring people along with them.

One of the original founders of DSCR, the late Tom Murchan, explained that he became involved in the project in the early 1980s because he believed that radio could provide a powerful communication channel for groups active in the community to promote themselves and to build the community:

I always felt that there was a tremendous need for some source for the local voluntary organisations to advertise themselves and disseminate their wares and so forth. I'm not a real radio buff, as such, but I felt that there was the need for this and that if we could possibly get it, it would be a marvellous source for the development of the community and that's really our purpose: the development of the community.

Their current chair, John O'Brennan, agrees, emphasising that south county Dublin did not have a strong tradition of community activism:

One of the advantages of the radio was to gather the community together. Unfortunately the history of Dundrum, around this area, is not great for community work and maybe people are a bit more affluent and it was a little bit separated. Community groups never got together and we were trying to draw them together and to use the station to disseminate knowledge and to get the groups together, to get them involved in the radio and to get people to listen to them and to see who they were.

Irish community radio stations find, over time, that the community development approach is a good way of working, although not all stations recognise that this, in effect, is what they are doing. Stations and aspirant stations should look to community development projects for ideas and if possible employ people with a community development background or, at the very least, people who are open to the principles and approach of community development practice. The community development process assists stations in evaluating and refining their practices. Likewise, community development workers should investigate the potential of community radio to enhance their own work. Community development and community radio, while not identical by any means, have much to offer the community when they work hand in hand.

6

Empowerment through Community Radio: NEAR Fm as Example

Sally Galiana and Ciarán Murray,
with an introduction by Jack Byrne

Introduction

There is much talk in the community and voluntary sector about "empowerment". Community radio stations need to come to an understanding of it in terms of a media role. Empowerment is not something that can be allocated or provided by anybody to anybody; empowerment, to be effective, must be a process of and for the self. People need information to create their own space, to define themselves and to gain confidence in unfolding their own identities for and by themselves, as more than consumers or voters.

Community stations which style themselves on the commercial hierarchy model make it difficult for local citizens to use this media space for empowerment dialogue. A community station seeking to be merely another radio service will leave itself little scope for innovative content development. Media owned and controlled by the local community offer an opportunity for those with very little power, not least communicative power, to confront the dominant communicative structure. Such a community service will select different themes and discourses. People, as

owners of this unique service, will actively design their own meaning system, which may well need to ignore or confront the meaning system of the burgeoning global social order.

Questions we asked ourselves, as we priced equipment back
in the early days, were: How could we assist people to become
active citizens rather than passive consumers? Is this, in fact, a
task for community radio? Should community radio see its content, the information, as a public good and not as a commodity?
Could we provide more in-depth analysis and contextualisation so
that people became informed enough to participate in public discourse? Wouldn't some of a station's listeners prefer information
along these lines? Would some listeners prefer to be left in
blessed peace? Or, would some listeners appreciate the empowerment of alternative worldviews? Surely, as a nation of talkers,
we could not try to put a muzzle on our local people in discourse? Of course, in the 1980s, we were not precocious enough
to use such language, but the sentiments were the same.

Ireland, like other societies, needs to develop more democratic public spheres, ones which are open to all citizens. Spaces
which enlarge citizen choice and which allow many different
voices to be heard, spaces where alternative viewpoints are on
offer to the public. A step-by-step deepening of this process of
public space needs to take place. The first step should be the provision of equal access to mediated public debate, and the second
could be the emergence of an unmediated appropriation of the
service by the local citizenry. This again requires that media practitioners acquire new media skills. And there is no use turning to
either of the other two sectors for assistance. They don't know
how to do media in this unique fashion. We have to devise our
own methods and practices. I believe that a community radio station can provide an important community service if it can devise
ways to provide this secure cultural space. For disempowerment
operates through the elimination of the local cultural space.
Whether a community will be able to develop its own cultural

identity so as to write its own agendas, rather than react to those of others, will depend on how well this space is provided.

So, a very useful service would be to provide a forum for local debate and for autonomous choice. To be a genuinely alternative space, it will have to deal with information not dealt with by other media, particularly by commercial media. Cultural globalisation, facilitated by technological innovations, supported by a liberal political climate, is leading rapidly to homogenised entertainment and mass marketing by a few mega-conglomerates. That is what will be on offer in Ireland as independent radios and television channels are bought up by bigger operators. Most commercial media owners in Ireland are not interested in their listeners or viewers except as advertising fodder and are quite happy to sell off their enterprises. Who then is really interested in the content of media in Ireland? Can community radio fill this void? Can we offer a real alternative to the bland, globalised cultural assault on our communities?

But how do we recognise a cultural space? I believe that it can refer to a community of interest, such as a college campus or a shared interest, say a language or religion. It can mean a geographical area, such as a town or a neighbourhood. A community station, in creating a cultural space, would be quite justified in attempting to stand still and reflect the present cultural norms of their locality. The problem is that their locale is being constantly bombarded and altered by outside media influences. Still, there is considerable merit in trying to defend what is. Other stations may wish to posit ideas about the environment and global human rights, so as to influence the community in what the station considers progressive ways. Two different approaches, but not mutually exclusive. It's possible that the optimum position for a community station is to ring-fence an agreed sector, a cultural space, and seek to defend its present values, while seeking to deepen and widen those values.

I'm sure that there are those who would claim that such an approach is contradictory, but if the cultural space is one where equality of access to the discourse is present, then that group, that community, can seek its own equilibrium. This cultural space should be a virtual space, with room for both conservative and progressive views. Provided the conservatives don't move to exclude other voices and the progressives don't sneer the more conservative into silence. A sense of genuine community needs to evolve in this space. The cultural space should leave room for the mentioning of things squeezed out by market media – such things as the spiritual side of our being, the sense of mutuality, the notion of equity, aesthetics and the interconnection between us and our planetary environment. In other words, our cultural space should be a celebration of the ecology of life in all its forms.

A new paradigm for communication that encourages self-empowerment cannot be driven by the state and it will not be facilitated by the market. It has to be initiated and sustained by civil society. Can community radio be the local voice of global civil society? If people as citizens of a civil society wish to be relieved of misinformation, of facile distractions and if they can no longer trust existing media to meet their needs, then an alternative medium surely has to provide a service of honest information, stimulating and relevant issues and the space for people to discuss this new knowledge. As a rule of thumb guide for community stations interested in such matters, in most countries civil society is legally rooted in sets of civil rights. And a station wishing to campaign on such issues should look to rights-based issues, allowing on air groups campaigning for such topics, and I'm sure most stations do this without even thinking about it. But an ad hoc approach leaves a station vulnerable to future down playing or the reduction of such activity. A community station could well attempt a form of codifying of some of these issues into a mission statement or set of objectives. Such a commitment could be to human rights, environmental protection and to support for civil society.

We sensed in the 1980s that a media culture had emerged that was making people powerless, as they become fodder for others, as consumers or as voters. A media culture of silence, where people could find no space or encouragement to speak on matters of concern or interest to them. A media culture that was violating the basic human right to communicate. These trends are even more visible today. To counter this, a real communications system is the key factor. Part of the self-empowerment process is that we shake free of the mesmerising influence of commercial media and we begin to sense the innate powers that we possess. We could then reply with Prospero in Shakespeare's *The Tempest*, "Now my charms are all o'erthrown, And what strength I have's mine own".

Empowerment through Community Radio

What makes community radio? Well, the answer could well be another question: what makes community? In some ways community is a balance of power, an exchange of information, a hub of relationships. Community radio should aspire to reproduce all of these components. Community radio should express the aspirations of civil society, especially those excluded from decision-making, by age, gender and from the economic arena. The only way of making it real is by opening doors and organisation structures to the participation of all those "cultures" that integrate in a society. Here the term "culture" tries to escape the corset of the geographical definition to become a living and changing expression of what society is. Culture is what we are, including our social class, neighbourhood, sexual orientation, abilities, gender and skin colour; every single aspect of what we are and which is often used to label and exclude individuals. So, community radio's function is to empower individuals and groups who have been left out of the loop by mainstream media, which is only interested in representing the middle classes with enough acquisitive power to satisfy the advertising agencies that pay for programming.

But what is empowerment? Empowerment refers to increasing the political, social or economic strength of individuals or groups. It often involves the empowered developing confidence in their capacities. Community radio work is often about the second part of this definition. Our role is to facilitate the development of confidence in their own capacities of those social groups that find themselves discriminated by power structures and society. This is why the training element is so important for community radio, as a way to develop not only skills, but also confidence in ourselves. And then, it is the even more important element of consultation, essential when it comes to produce relevant and really participative empowerment processes.

So far, this is the theory, but how does it work in practice? Is it possible to do what the theory suggests? And more importantly, do we want to be empowered? The following are a series of examples taken from projects run by NEAR Fm over the past ten years that illustrate the work our community radio station does with all the many and various cultures represented in our society. To facilitate the reader, they are presented under different headings: Youth, New Immigrants and Refugees, Ex-prisoners, Travellers, Ability and the Unemployed.

Youth

It can be difficult to empower anyone without being patronising and this is even truer in the case of young people than with other age groups. It is relatively easy to get a few teenagers behind a microphone and to let them play pop music, but to get them to do something more is difficult. We have wrestled with the question over the years as to whether or not they want to do more. Or perhaps, all they want to do is to play pop music? But if you work at it and get them to try talk programming such as current affairs, debating or drama, it is surprising and inspiring what they come up with. We have had several attempts over the years at creating youth programming. Working with some very dedicated people we have had a few NEAR Fm "youth clubs".

NEAR Fm does not run competitions, as we believe the world is competitive enough already. Most competitions aimed at young people, for writing the best story for example, reward those who are in receipt of many accolades anyway. However there are times to bend the rules and in 1998 and 1999 we ran the schools' debate challenge. We ran these live and outdoors to add to the occasion. We brought in a panel of independent judges, and rather than rewarding the winners of the debates *per se,* the "winners" were those who put the most into it. This led to an incident where one rather infamous school with a poor reputation beat a "good" school, considered locally as a model of good education practices. The so-called "good school" teacher stormed off in disgust. We had however equal prizes for all pupils for taking part and a party afterwards. Some of the teenagers remained involved making programmes and one is now a member of our management committee.

Pre-teens can be a lot of fun, being far less self-conscious than teenagers and their imaginations are as yet unfettered by life. Capturing some of this magic is very special and one project in particular serves as a good example of where we managed to do that. Chris Gavin worked on radio drama with 8- to10-year-olds, some of whom were experiencing difficulties at school. We discussed ideas for radio plays and they came up with "Aliens and Broccoli". With some rehearsals and a lot of ad-libbing the pre-teens came up with some wonderfully chaotic pieces of audio full of bizarre humour that raced along at a frightening pace.

When you are involved with the community in making programmes, it can often be the case that, where you have concerns about the content, then you are probably getting close to empowerment. After some basic production and presentation skills training we let some teenagers go it alone. We ran a workshop

on how discussion programmes might, just might, be as interesting as music. What they came up with was not what we expected.
For example, the programme on teenage drink featured a teen-
ager saying that he thought binge drinking was really stupid (so far
so good), but went on to explain how the illegal drug ecstasy was
much better and recommended it as a far superior alternative to
drinking! That made people think, and made the programming
committee dance. The old chestnuts of censorship, control and
mediation all come into play on every medium.

New Immigrants and Refugees

When Bosnian refugees came to Dublin in 1994 and 1995 from
war-torn Yugoslavia we contacted them to see if we could be of
any help. They were interested in the idea of a radio programme
in their own language as most of them did not speak English. We
gave some basic training in production and presentation and then
they were ready to go. They used the weekly programme to give
news of missing friends and relatives and they broadcast requests
and dedications to the Bosnians living here and gave details of parties and gatherings. These programmes were also broadcast on
Tallaght Community Radio (TCR) as there were Bosnians living in
that part of the city too.

   We at NEAR Fm learned a little Serbo-Croat and met first-
hand people we would usually only see on television. The Bosnians came to our parties and we went to theirs. After the war in
former Yugoslavia was over many Bosnians returned home. By
1998 the Bosnians who remained had less need of a programme
in Serbo-Croat and the programme ended, but we remained in
contact and worked together on subsequent projects. The experience we gained helped us to welcome those who came to our
shores more recently.

   Unlike the Bosnians, who were legal, UN-sanctioned refugees,
those who came later, had a more difficult time. The year 1998
was a bad one for immigrants in Ireland and for refugees in par-

ticular. The mainstream media was full of scare stories about floods of immigrants coming to Ireland and there had been some racially-motivated attacks. We wanted to do something. We organised a meeting in the Vietnamese Centre in the north inner city, inviting refugees, immigrant groups and NGOs to come along. The turnout was good with perhaps 25 groups there and after some discussion we agreed on the idea of "Refugee Radio". NEAR Fm would hand over its complete schedule and operation for one week to the refugees.

Some of the NEAR Fm committee of management were a bit taken aback and wondered if Sally and Ciarán as station managers would be taking a week's holiday. The reality was quite the opposite of course. We began an extensive consultation and training period. Empowerment in practice is multi-layered and many who agreed to make programmes were less interested in going on a management committee to draw up a schedule, to do the publicity and to make the tea. A few hardy fools were selected and Kensika Monshengwo, of the Irish Refugee Council, and Remi Agwobosoro, from Nigeria, were instrumental in bringing the whole thing together. The programming ideas came from the groups themselves. Most of the programmes were in English as this was seen as a way to reach as wide an audience as possible. Some wanted to do overtly political programmes, others kept to world music formats. More wanted a very positive spin on their country and the example of Rwanda comes to mind. The event being a short time after the genocide there, it was unusual to hear stories of the beauty of the landscape and the fame of the musical tradition there. On another programme about the Ivory Coast the wonderful beach life was discussed and the volleyball and surfing sounded more like Bondi Beach in Australia than the usual European impressions of Africa.

The Nigerians wanted a phone-in where they would be in-charge of the microphone, turning the usual rightwing zoo radio phone-shows on their head. We were a little concerned at this, as it wasn't part of our usual format and we could see the potential for it to go wrong. However, if you want to empower people, it has to be to let them have the power to get it wrong too. It went very well and Áine Ní Chonaill, a high profile, anti-immigration spokesperson from a group known as the Irish Immigration Control Platform rang in to argue her case with Remi. She was unhappy that so much airtime was given to refugees and threatened to complain to the Broadcasting Complaints Commission of Ireland. A public seminar was held in the home of Dublin's Lord Mayor, the Mansion House. This venue was chosen because of its symbolical importance as site of the first independent Irish Parliament and historical seat of power in Dublin. The panel was partly made up of refugees and the issues of the day were debated with a lively audience. The whole project caught the attention of the mainstream media. Most of the national dailies carried articles with photos of black faces hosting radio programmes and mainstream radio and TV stations carried the story on their main current affairs programmes.

Some of the refugees stayed on at NEAR Fm after "Refugee Radio" week to make regular programmes and to become part of the fabric of NEAR Fm itself. Many were not eligible at that time to work or to study in their new country and had time on their hands. Since then, we have supported many refugees in getting their proper legal status and working permits. We believe that by throwing open our schedule and resources we were able to offer something approaching genuine empowerment. Refugee Radio week was a success in various ways. Refugees were trained in radio production, but more importantly they had a voice — a voice as a presenter, not merely as a guest, and this at a time when there were many racist articles and features in the media. This gave them the opportunity to tell their stories and to confront some of the racist views. Volunteers and staff in NEAR Fm also benefited. For many it was their first time meeting Africans, let alone refugees. One volunteer asked a Nigerian why he came to

Ireland and the refugee showed him a bullet wound and explained that he was fleeing for his life. Also for volunteers it was a chance to express their own anti-racism views and it provided them with a platform to support the refugees.

We made friends and won trust and that trust has grown and borne much fruit. Today we are working as a partner with some of the same people, and with many new ones, on an application for a multicultural licence for Dublin. NEAR Fm is acting in an advisory capacity because we believe that a multicultural licence should have a multicultural ownership and that this ownership should be democratic.

Ex-prisoners

In 1997 we decided to work with recently released prisoners to see if we could help in their reintegration into society. We did this because many of the inmates of Dublin's Mountjoy jail come from working class estates and flats within our catchment area. There is also a hostel for recently released prisoners in Priorswood, a stone's throw from the station, and the training centre and workshops for ex-prisoners are located nearby in Santry.

We designed a project that would involve training 12 recently-released prisoners in radio production. Our plan was that they would make three radio programmes, "Before Prison", "In Prison" and "After Prison". We applied for and received £1,700 from the Jesuit Foundation and engaged a trainer, Louis LeRooski. As a trainer Louis seemed to have an inherent grasp of empowerment as a process and a lot of personal patience. He would allow trainees to get things wrong again and again and still he would persevere until he had trained people we had almost given up on as untrainable.

Louis and Ciarán met with some recent ex-prisoners from Mountjoy who did training in PACE, an organisation for recently released prisoners in their training centre in Santry. Some of the trainees were still in prison and were attending training on day-release and the Department of Justice seemed to forbid these prisoners from talking about prison conditions. This concerned us and we were considering the legality of the Department's position. But, more importantly, the prisoners and ex-prisoners didn't want to talk about prison, saying it was boring and depressing. At this point we realised that we had decided what ex-prisoners might like to make programmes about without asking them. As a first step, empowerment is about enabling people to do what they want to do, and so we did.

They decided that they wanted to do programmes about football and Bob Marley and one on joy-riding. The training went quite well and they were interested and learned quickly. We didn't tell staff or volunteers who they were so they were treated quite normally and people didn't watch their handbags all day long. After the training, when we told the staff and volunteers that that group of trainees were ex-prisoners, they were generally surprised and said how normal they had seemed. Upon reflection this may have been a bit patronising on our part, but it was done in an attempt to integrate people without bringing them under the cloud of suspicion.

The recordings on joy-riding were very powerful. Only at this stage did we realise that the man making these programmes was still in Mountjoy Prison, doing our training on day-release. He would search for "joy-riders", wave them down and interview them in stolen cars. They explained joy-riding as a game, saying they didn't care about anyone's property. He cautioned them about ending up like him and they said they didn't care about that either. One day after the course had finished, Mountjoy Prison rang to ask if he was training with us. He wasn't and it seems they had believed him when he said he was leaving prison to do training with us. Later we met with a parole officer from Mountjoy Prison who apologised to us over the incident, but we also failed here insofar as we didn't know enough about the people we were working with. Sometimes too much emphasis can be put on training and programming and not enough on working with the whole person in the reality of their own world.

Overall, it was an important lesson in empowerment for us. Ciarán's personal interest in the stories that ex-prisoners might have to tell was decided upon without asking them their opinion. We've tried to remedy that. Also, the training course itself was fine but it did not have any continuity built in to it and a few weeks after the training these people had vanished from NEAR Fm. When we look at projects now we try to think how they can be sustained. Empowerment needs to thought of as having a time factor. Once-off training and programming do not really amount to empowerment as the people are left hanging at the end of a project and the sustainability of working with a group has to be built in from the start.

Travellers

NEAR Fm's catchment area, Dublin North-East, holds the highest percentage of Travellers in the capital city. From the inception of the station, the Travelling community has been one of the focus groups for many of our programmes and projects. During the years we have come to build a very strong relationship with Pavee Point, the Travellers' Cultural Centre in Dublin, producing various documentaries on Traveller culture and social discrimination against members of this community. We have also broadcast live a couple of discussion programmes from Pavee Point, North Charles Street, in Dublin's north inner city. Others areas of programming have also worked with Travellers, so their opinions and perspectives in issues of relevance to their community could be heard by the settled community.

This relationship has lead to NEAR Fm and Pavee Point working as partners on a couple of projects. For example, Pavee Point applied to produce a series of programmes in partnership with NEAR Fm under Development Co-operation Ireland's (DCI) Challenge Fund. More recently, Pavee Point has been one of the organisations applying to the BCI for a multicultural radio licence under the community of interest category. And although this initial application was not successful, Pavee Point wants to work towards a future application for a multicultural radio station because Travellers feel they will never get a fair hearing or their proper voice on commercial or national media. They believe that community radio is the right model for social groups that are being marginalised and deprived of their right to communicate. This is why they will be availing of CRAOL/FETAC training for their own volunteers (see Chapters 4 and 11).

Ability

Working for people with disabilities shows how negative we are in our approach to those who we deem "different". For staff at NEAR Fm who have the opportunity to work with people with disabilities, the mental barriers and prejudices are fading. Working on radio is about abilities, and all members of staff and volunteers have shown they have plenty of skills over the years.

Being a Community Employment (CE) Project, many members of NEAR Fm staff are in receipt of some kind of disability payment. Our experience has been that the input and effort of many very different individuals enriches our project and our output and makes NEAR Fm the unique organisation that it is.

The premises of NEAR Fm have been accessible to wheelchair users since 1997, and this facilitates the production of a radio programme by clients of the Central Remedial Clinic, who have also availed of our training. Visually impaired people have been part of our volunteer body from the beginning of the station. In collaboration with the National Council for the Blind, Braille indications were provided for the use of our sound desk. We also run special broadcasts, round-table discussions and provide news of developments relevant to people with disabilities.

Community is about living, sharing and working together and NEAR Fm tries to reflect the community as a whole in the body of volunteers and staff. And the same goes for abilities. We feel everyone is entitled to have a voice and to develop their areas of interest, without prejudices dictating what role they should take on. Community is also about learning from each other and the so-called "able" have also learnt a lot about the capabilities of people with "disabilities".

The Unemployed

NEAR Fm is located in an area of high unemployment. The Principal Economic Status figures from the Census of 2002 show that unemployment in Dublin North Central – which is part of our catchment area – is at 8.2 per cent, representing about 19.9 per cent of Dublin City's unemployment population. The Media Co-op is responsible for the running of a Community Employment (CE) project. This means that most of the staff are recruited from the ranks of the long-term unemployed and that staff turnover is quite high, as the CE scheme only allows for individuals over 35 years to participate for a maximum of three years and younger people can usually only stay with the project for a year. This means that people who are trained and are responsible for areas of programming will leave at some stage. On the other hand, it keeps us on our toes, and it forces us to make training central to our strategic plans, providing participants with skills, a work context, building their pride in their contribution to society, and most importantly, a voice to air the issues they consider relevant and important. For staff on the CE scheme it is important also to move into paid employment from a financial point of view.

Obviously, from the point of view of the government agency FÁS, the CE scheme is a stepping stone in the progression of the programme participants towards "real" employment. From our point of view, all CE participants are workers – they sign a contract when joining and they are given responsibility over areas of programming or production. They take editorial decisions on the content of the programme, production decisions. Staff are consulted on any matter relevant to them arising in the running of the station. They hold their staff meetings and their staff representative will bring matters to management's attention. Members of staff have been invited to attend management committee meetings and to become shareholders of the Co-op. When they finish their employment with us, they are invited to become volunteers and if they decide to do so, they can become members of the management committee themselves.

So far, the CE experience has been very positive for NEAR Fm and also for the CE participants themselves. It seems that a wealth of skills remain outside the work market just because they cannot be measured by the very narrow rules of commercial enterprise, like creativity, for example. Interest in your community does not score very high either. But mostly it is because mainstream media are not interested in training and developing their staff and they have placed the idea of previous experience as a disqualifying rule against many newcomers into journalism. However, we are interested in creativity and in community work because it is part of our ethos. Empowerment is a primary goal for us. Previous experience is not required to join NEAR Fm; in fact, training is compulsory for anyone joining the ranks of our volunteers or staff.

Our project has enabled people to find their feet when it comes to further education and employment. Some of our staff decided to go back to full-time education, most of them in areas related to the traditional mass media or newer multimedia. Other staff and volunteers have found jobs in the commercial media sector in diverse areas, from administration to research. Many CE participants who wished to remain with NEAR Fm secured Job Initiative positions through FÁS that allow them to continue their involvement with community media on a paid basis.

Through their involvement in community media, previously unemployed people have widened their social networks considerably, often adding local politicians, community workers, government ministers, and senior civil servants to their contacts. This has demystified the role and responsibility of statutory bodies, learning about their rights and duties as citizens, and becoming vocal in the criticism of social and political structures. Most importantly, at a time where media is overpowering, where information is not objective anymore, they have reached an understanding of how media works, the values it promotes, and what it leaves behind or ignores. It enables the previously unemployed to taste the value of their rights as citizens and they exercise them in a very direct way, appealing and challenging politicians and statutory bodies in new ways.

Conclusions

We tried to define empowerment as the development of people's confidence in their own capacities for those in social groups that find themselves discriminated against by power structures and by society. However, the empowerment processes are as important as the final aims of strength and capacity for individual and communal action. Through our own experiences we have learned to consult more with groups and individuals about what they want to achieve instead of coming up with interesting but flawed ideas of how to empower them. This is particularly evident with regard to our experience with the PACE programme. There was not a lot of consultation at the beginning of the project. It was set up by their probation officer and by our trainers, but there was little contact with the training participants themselves until they had arrived at the studios. Obviously, what they expected was not what they got, and we struggled to finish the training. We anticipated working with 12 participants, started with five and only two completed the project, producing a short package on joy-riding. As we said, empowerment is about developing confidence in the people with whom we are working, but we have also learned that it is about building trust. We feel that many of the groups and individuals that have worked with us over the years have developed great confidence in their capacities and skills, but we also believe that we have won a level of trust with many groups who are normally suspicious of the media such as immigrants and Travellers. In these relationships, groups have evolved from being users of a service to being partners in providing information and entertainment. This new partnership relationship can be seen in the multicultural radio project, whereby immigrants and Travellers have the confidence to develop their own station.

This trust has not come easily. Gaining the trust of marginalised people is a result of long term co-operation, up to 10 years in some cases. Their proximity to the radio, their constant presence at the studios and at the end of the phone line, their contact with our volunteers and staff have also reinforced their confidence in themselves and their communication skills. We try to get them to use community radio as a resource. The next step has been to make them understand that we provide them with the possibility for them to become subjects, owners and editors of the media – in short, to become the authors and not the subjects.

Finally, empowerment is also about demystifying media, and demonstrating to our many partners the strength of the community element in community radio. Often people have preconceived, hegemonic ideas of what radio is and how it works that interfere with a community group's use of their media. Part and parcel of our aim of empowering people is getting other organisations to know us and to meet us. This allows us to learn from other organisations, to read their strategic plans, their missions and visions, to invite community groups to take part on radio programmes as guests to explain the work they do and their aspirations, and to find ways in which community radio can work with them.

Then, there is also the training element. Insisting that people undergo training may seem patronising but it provides the opportunity to explain what community radio is and what it can be. This gives them the confidence to see radio as more than a medium for pop music and competitions. It opens the door to a more creative and innovative role for the medium. This is especially relevant for CE scheme participants and long-term unemployed people, who after training and some hands-on experience become the head of current affairs, or responsible for the studios, or the trainers of the next wave of recruits. The same holds true for some of the youth training projects, which may have started in a mainstream vein and went on to make very creative, talk-based programming.

In conclusion, this is the NEAR Fm experience. The answers provided by the preceding vignettes are not straightforward, and clearly not universal, but hopefully they shed some light and point to what not to do as much as what to do when it comes to empowerment.

7

Women in Irish Community Radio

Nessa McGann

Part of the work of community radio is to develop people to their full potential and in doing so raise the capability of the community as a whole. As a tool for community development community radio seeks to combat disadvantage in our communities, to break down prejudices and to find, support and celebrate the positive in our society. Many of the minority groups targeted by community radio are marginalised by both mainstream media and society in general, for example older people, Travellers, early school leavers, the disabled and ethnic minorities. Community radio aims to provide a space where the members of these communities have access to training and can participate in the power structures and day-to-day output of the radio station. The following chapter draws on research conducted in 2003–2004 where I examined the facilitation by two community radio stations of the participation and empowerment of one particular group who face a double-edged sword in terms of discrimination and marginalisation in society – women.

My research on the participation and empowerment of women through community radio took place between 2002 and 2003 and was the basis for my MA thesis (McGann, 2003). It focused on two case studies, a rural station licensed in 1998, Radio

Corca Baiscinn (RCB), and an urban station, licensed as part of the original pilot project in 1994, NEAR Fm. I conducted interviews with staff, management and volunteers from both stations and this chapter draws on those interviews and on documentary evidence regarding the role of women in Irish society on the community radio policy of the Irish radio regulatory body (Broadcast Commission of Ireland, BCI). I also examined each station's training and broadcast schedule as well as their own documented commitments to enabling women's access to and participation in the radio station. Both station managers are named but other respondents are not to protect their privacy.

The National Women's Council of Ireland (NWCI) define poverty as "not just the absence of income and physical resources, but also exclusion from participation in society, lack of power, and unequal distribution of resources" (NWCI, 2006). This is the type of poverty that community radio, through its democratic means of communication, its commitment to access and participation in the structures of the radio station and its mandate to represent the concerns of the community, seeks to overcome. These fundamental principles of Irish community radio are enshrined in the AMARC Europe Charter for community radio (see appendix).

Recent research conducted by the NWCI on women and poverty tells us that Irish women are at a higher risk of poverty than Irish men. Households headed by someone "working full-time in the home" form the largest income poverty group – this group is composed predominantly of women. The research shows that carers, those on the minimum wage, lone parents, households headed by someone working full-time in the home or by an older person, all experience greater poverty than the demographic "norm" – and these groups all have women in the majority. The NWCI research clearly demonstrates that:

> While women's experience of poverty has certain features
> common to all groups, it also covers a wide range of diverse
> experiences for differing groups of women. The effects of
> multiple discrimination create additional obstacles inhibiting
> an escape from poverty (NWCI, 2006).

In other words: the double-edged sword.

Throughout our society, women are unequally represented in positions of power. In a situation where more than half of those earning below the minimum wage are women (NWCI, 2006), it is not surprising that there are far more men than women at senior management level. With regard to the numbers of women in parliament around the world, Ireland ranks in joint 63rd place with Barbados (IPU, 2006).

Think of your local radio station or any national radio station you may be familiar with. Who are the voices of the radio station? Who are the main representatives of your local station? Without a doubt a small number of extremely well-known women have high profile jobs as presenters in some national stations – but the majority of presenters on national and local stations are men. If you look more closely at the station structures and ask who manages the radio stations, then the imbalance in gender representation is starker still – of the 27 local commercial stations broadcasting in Ireland in 2006 – only one station (Tipp FM) is run by a female CEO. In contrast, of the 19 licensed community radio stations broadcasting that year, eight station managers are female. Therefore, it is evident that, while gender imbalance exists in both types of independent radio in Ireland, community radio stations have been more successful in moving towards a balanced representation of women in positions of organisational power.

I joined community radio as a volunteer in Cork Campus Radio – managed at that time by Sinéad Wylde – around the time that employment and gender patterns were beginning to be examined by a number of actors in Irish independent radio. In 1998 the first research on employment and gender was published, *Breaking*

Glass Walls – Employment and Gender Patterns in Independent Radio in Ireland (Gibbons, 1998). This was conducted by Dr. Maria Gibbons and Nexus Research and was funded by the Women-On-Air project – a joint initiative of the then IRTC (now BCI), University College Galway (now NUI, Galway) and Connemara Community Radio. This research found that 52 per cent of community radio employees and 40 per cent of board members were female. This is in comparison to the situation in commercial radio where 41 per cent of all employees and 14 per cent of board members were female. The research also showed that only 5 per cent of top executives and 39 per cent of middle management working in commercial radio were female. At the time, these figures contrasted starkly with community radio, where 70 per cent of those employed at management/administrative level were women.

It was interesting to note the difference between representation of women on boards of management – why was the level of participation in community radio management so high? However upon closer examination, it became clear that community radio stations in Ireland are required by contract to have a 40 per cent minimum membership of women on their boards. This clause was introduced as part of the discussions by the Community Radio Forum of Ireland (CRF, or the Forum, see Chapters 3 and 4) during 1995–1997 which developed into the community radio policy adopted by the BCI. This quota does not exist for Irish commercial stations.

Many women are uncomfortable with the sort of positive discrimination implicit in such arrangements, while others have highlighted the fact that they merely counterbalance the implicit positive discrimination in favour of men that has become the norm. Some see these quotas as structurally critical to the continued participation of women at crucial levels of operation. However, in the Irish context, this decision, by those engaged in the pilot project, to ensure representation by women in senior management positions and as board members in community radio, sprang from the historical origins and links to the principles and processes inherent in community development. In the course of my research on female participation in community radio, practitioners directly linked the importance of gender balance in all structures of the radio to the influence of the Irish community development movement.

The station manager of the rural case study, Niamh Farren, noted that the decision to have a 50/50 gender balance on their board of management was directly related to the community development focus of the original "parent" or sponsor organisation – a rural development agency particularly dedicated to supporting the development, training and participation of women in local society. She observed that women were high up on the list of priorities for the original group who applied for the license. Farren also spoke about the history of the station and said that from the beginning, RCB has involved the women from the area who were already community activists and that an original aim of the station was the inclusion of women in every area of the station:

> Going back to when we were setting up the station, [women were one of] the groups we wanted to benefit so it's a complete contradiction if you don't push that at a management level because, from what I've read about community radio, it's very good at facilitating certain groups in programming, but when it comes to them being in a decision making role, then it comes back to a certain group, so we would be quite conscious of that.

Training is a key component of the work of community radio stations and the commitment to providing high quality training for participants and staff has been central in the development of the Irish community radio movement. The provision of skills to marginalised or otherwise excluded members of the community is also a global aim of community radio (see AMARC Europe Charter in appendix) and was a core component of the work that both

RCB and NEAR Fm engaged in. Crucially, training and skills development of marginalised members of society is also central to the concept of Community Employment (CE) schemes which at the time of research provided the majority of general staff workers for community radio stations.

A founding member of the board of RCB commented that the education or training element in community radio drew women to the station in the early stages. In addition, she noted the lack of real and meaningful work for women in the local area, a place where career options for all who live in the Loop Head Peninsula, especially women, were extremely limited:

> When the station was being set up, the only CE schemes available in the area were manual labour based such as grave and ditch digging and really favoured the employment of men.

Training offered to women and men in these stations is on a formal and informal "mentoring/shadowing" basis. In both stations, participants had asked for, and been provided with, "women only" training courses. In NEAR Fm this need was identified on a case-by-case basis and provided wherever it was requested by participants and management. This situation was mirrored in RCB, where training courses in community radio and technology, including transmission, editing and production skills, were provided by a female trainer as participants felt more at ease in that situation.

Training offered in both stations focused initially on community radio training, introducing the ethos and history of the global community radio movement, the principles which link community radio to community development and the AMARC Europe Charter (see appendix). Other training offered by the stations included computer skills, personal development opportunities, administration skills and programme production techniques. At the time of research, NEAR Fm had developed a higher level of training and courses offered included current affairs training, programming, book and film reviewing and, crucially, a module in training for trainers. Without participation in the radio, these training opportunities would have been out of the reach of the participants.

However, it is interesting to note that, at the time of research, all the participants at the training for trainer's course in NEAR Fm were men. It is particularly disappointing given that my research found that training sessions delivered to volunteers by men only did not encourage full and equal participation of women in the life of the station. Since this research was carried out a number of training for trainer courses have been delivered through the Community Radio Support Scheme (CRSS, see Chapter 4). These are facilitated by CRAOL – the national network for training, development and representation of community radio in Ireland (see Chapter 4). These accredited courses were run in 2003 and 2004 with a 2:1 ratio of female to male participants attending and all of the women who attended the course received full accreditation. In this context it is also interesting to note that the annual Community Radio Training Féile (see Chapter 4) has been instigated and largely run by female station managers and female station training officers. The first six Féilte in Clare, Galway, Cork, Dublin, Limerick and Donegal were all run by female station managers. The sub-groups supporting this process have been staffed almost exclusively (with the exceptions of the Cork- and Dublin-based stations) by female volunteers and members of staff.

While the full impact of female organisation and participation in these national courses and events has yet to be measured by CRAOL, a number of key questions arise. Is Irish community radio unusual in having such a high level of female participation in the design, delivery and implementation of training events and strategies? What are the factors that facilitate this high level of participation by women? Why is there such a high level of female trainers in the sector and is this reflected in other broadcasting sectors? Are female participants in Irish community radio more at ease in a training role? How does this influence participation in training in their own stations and in the sector as a whole?

There are a number of factors which prohibit the engagement of women in training and these are directly related to the high cost of training, lack of information about training opportunities and the low self-confidence of the participants. However, while these factors work to inhibit access to training, the possibility of accessing training gives many women participants in community radio the impetus to overcome physical and logistical difficulties. As Farren reported:

> I've had women hitching in and out from Kilrush to get into work ever since I've started here, it certainly hasn't stopped anyone from working here, but that's how great [the women] are, in the December grey weather, leaving their kids off at whatever kind of childcare facility they can get and coming up to work.

The research I undertook clearly demonstrates that the level and areas of participation by women in the life of the station are directly related to the levels of training offered to female participants. Thus, the station which facilitated women who had been out of the workforce, many with low educational achievements, to train in so-called "soft skills", such as literacy, leadership and personal development, in addition to production and technical skills training, such as radio production, editing, studio engineering, resulted in a higher number of women working in non-traditional roles within the radio station for example as station engineers and as editors.

While CRAOL is doing much to meet the obvious interest women have shown in developing their skills base, the position of women as trainers and the importance of training a core component of community radio could be re-examined in the light of previous initiatives such as Training for Trainers and the CRAOL subgroup structure. There is also, I believe, a need for an audit of training and the levels of participation by women and men in individual station training courses. Such information would be particularly invaluable to the future development of the community radio movement.

While training is a key element of the work of the radio as a community development project, programming is the key element of the work of any station, whether it is a state, commercial, pirate or community radio broadcaster. Programming provided by a station is the clearest indicator of the ethos, the ideals and the motivation behind the radio service. The mass media influences how people construct and reflect the society in which they live, Yet the voices, concerns and experiences of women are not represented on the traditional mass media as equally as those of men. So how does community radio differ from mainstream media in terms of its programming policies and outputs? How do women fare throughout the general station programming? Do community radio stations feature specific programming for women, modelled on the well known BBC Radio 4 programme the *Women's Hour*? What good would such programmes do? How do the women involved in community radio programming feel about these issues?

In general, women carry out a wide variety of roles within Irish community radio stations. These positions are held in areas such as general management, technical, programming and administration. Some female participants in community radio act as volunteers; others hold full or part-time paid positions. The main areas in community radio in which women have been found to work have been 30 per cent in programming, 24 per cent in technical areas while 17 per cent of women work in office and secretarial jobs (Gibbons, 1998).

In NEAR Fm, the more established urban station, programming was at a more advanced stage and their hours of broadcasting were far in excess of those of the rural station. However, in both stations, women contributed to programme making in a number of ways, as programme producers, presenters, editors, technicians and researchers. There was a higher number of female to male presenters in RCB, the rural radio station, than in the urban station. This can be directly linked to the focused intake of female participants and the ethos of the local development company. At the time of my research, RCB employed ten people on a part-time basis and a full-time station manager through the CE scheme. Seventy per cent of the CE staff were women; indeed the station has had a long history of employing women from the area in significant numbers. It was notable that two of these women are involved in administration, but both also contribute to programming on an ongoing basis, particularly to women's programming, and they are encouraged to participate in radio training. Providing training and employment opportunities for local people was also undertaken in NEAR Fm through its involvement with the CE scheme. At the time of my research, the station employed 15 participants, seven of whom were women. Of these, one participant worked in administration and in programme research and three participants worked exclusively in administration. The other three worked in programming. In addition to this, four full-time workers are employed by the associated Media Co-op and these all also participate in the running of the radio station. Both stations studied were in favour of equal access to programme making by both men and women. However, neither station specified that they promoted women as programme-makers; rather both stations committed themselves to providing access to the airwaves for members of disenfranchised groups of their communities, including those who have little or no access to mainstream media.

The format of the *Women's Hour* programme in both stations is worth comparing. While the older, urban station had previously broadcast such a programme, their *Women's Hour* had then morphed into a programme based around general equality issues. This change in title and focus had happened for a number of reasons, mainly due to the movement of presenters within the station and the perceived need for a more generally based "rights and equality issues" programme. It was made clear that a programme dealing specifically with women's issues would be supported by station management and that it could be very relevant to the community, but that it was the prerogative of the women in the station to initiate the programme. A male member of management commented:

> I think that it [Women's Issues programme] is a good idea. I think that it is up to women; I don't want to make that decision [to produce a women's hour programme] on behalf of women. We did have a women's programme, but we collapsed it into the equality programme, to a certain degree for a lack of material

A certain level of debate exists in media and communication studies (Baehr, 1980) about the impact of the *Women's Hour* programming – does it further serve to ghettoise women within the general broadcast schedule or does it provide a valuable opportunity to focus on issues that affect women? If one hour a day is devoted to women, does this mean that the other 23 are just for men? Are the broadcasters of the *Women's Hour* programme now working to exclude men from a part of the programme schedule?

A participant interviewed at the rural station answered this question when she observed that the *Women's Hour* programme did not exclude men, but rather deals with topics in a way that they are not dealt with on other programmes. She observed that:

> [The women's hour] has changed a lot – if you are talking around women and women's issues, some of [those issues] are around men and men should be involved, to have their say ... I invited a man in to talk about the break up of his marriage [and then] men came in and spoke on women drivers ...

This view was echoed by another participant, who reflected that the programme discussed issues which affected everyone, not just women. She observed that while the programme is researched, produced, presented and broadcast by a woman-only team, men are interviewed as well. Participants at both stations noted that the presence of women as researchers, technicians, presenters and producers enabled station programmes to transmit the views and voices of women. In particular, the station manager of the rural station felt that the *Women's Hour* suited their schedule, and commented that once women had roles in producing other programmes, then it didn't ghettoise them.

So it emerged that for a younger station, with a less developed programme schedule, but supported by a local development organisation fuelled by the ethos of supporting the inclusion of women's issues into the mainstream media, such a programme proved extremely important. During my research, many staff and volunteers in RCB commented that they needed more time to adequately address issues raised during the *Women's Hour* programme (it was broadcast for two hours every week). They noted that this need to expand the programme was due to the diverse nature of the programme material, where presenters cover extremely serious and very light-hearted topics in quick succession. An example of this was when a participant spoke to me about an interview on lingerie she conducted. This unexpectedly turned from a very insubstantial interview on buying underwear into a serious discussion on wearing breast prostheses and the self image of older women and women who have experienced breast cancer.

For this participant, this example highlighted the importance of the *Women's Hour* programme and the relevance of the rural radio station to the local community. As she observed, "The current affairs show won't change the world, but the *Women's Hour* might!"

While this view may be overstated, it is a great indicator of the self-belief expressed by the female participants interviewed during my research. The confidence and assurance in the relevance and significance of their contribution to the radio station was a common factor for all involved in the research.

The similarity in opinions expressed by both female station managers in terms of their job satisfaction is noteworthy. In spite of the considerable workload experienced by both managers, they expressed high levels of job satisfaction. These related to the challenges of the job, the satisfaction with producing good programmes and the fact that community radio is constantly evolving. Farren, the manager of RCB, commented:

> It really is the most challenging work ... Its never boring, I have enjoyed working with different groups in the community ... one that sticks out is a group of people with learning disabilities, that's the thing that I am most proud of ... just getting that group to the stage where they put together a radio programme.

This ability of the radio station to directly influence the lives of the people who participate in the life of the station was echoed by the manager of NEAR Fm, Galliano, when she observed that:

> When you come in in the morning you could end up talking about fashion, then you start talking about politics, so it's not only a place to work but also a place to change, where you can develop ideas and opinions, that's what I really like.

While both female managers were satisfied generally with their work, they did list some difficulties inherent in the job of manager. These mainly centred on the difficulties faced when participants have to leave the station because their CE scheme has finished. Farren reported that it was very distressing to have to let people go just because they are finished on the CE scheme: "Then just with the whole FÁS thing, its very frustrating when people leave after a year and it's very upsetting". Galliano echoed this, when she remarked on the most frustrating part of her job: "When I have to let go people that are very valuable to the station, that's when people are on community employment, that's one of the worst things."

The similarities expressed by the station managers were mirrored in the comments by participants with social interaction a key factor in adding to job satisfaction for all. This is in part due to the fact that all those employed in the CE schemes have been excluded from the workforce, for whatever reason, for some time. A participant in NEAR Fm commented that real and meaningful interaction with others is central to her job satisfaction:

> It's great to get out and interact …You'd sit and have a conversation about the Iraqi war and everyone will get involved in it. It doesn't interfere with your work, but it adds to it and you'd say "God, we had a great day today".

Participants in the rural station echoed this observation. One woman observed that she herself has developed a sense of self-confidence and is learning how to deal with people in a work situation again. Another pointed out that she had made friends with her colleagues and that these are people who live in the same area, but who she wouldn't necessarily have met, other than through her involvement with the station. This ties in well with the ethos of community radio stations, which aim to counter the marginalisation and isolation felt by members of their community.

As a community radio station manager and a working mother I have always been interested in the perceptions, policies relating to and the roles adopted by women in the media but especially those women who work and volunteer in community radio. Believing that women's voices are seriously underrepresented in media, as producers, presenters and as technicians, I undertook the research briefly outlined above. So what did I find? Does Irish community radio facilitate the access, participation and empowerment of women?

And the answer is, of course, yes and no. I found that the initial support from organisations which believe in gender equality is extremely helpful in creating a community radio culture where equality is the norm. I found that management structures of the community radio station must provide for and ensure gender equality in all areas of station life on an ongoing basis. I found that training is a real indicator of the state of gender equality in any community radio station and this is influenced by the station itself as well as by the national community radio context in which it operates. I found that programming specifically targeted at women's issues can and does occur and that if this suits the needs of the community then it should be supported and continued. Most critically, I also found that women working, as staff and as volunteers in community radio stations, really value the experience for training, for education and for the opportunity to build their sense of self worth and to connect with their community on an equal basis – through their involvement in community radio.

8

Adult Education through Community Radio: The Example of Community Radio Castlebar

Pat Stanton

When commercial radio licences were offered to operators in the late 1980s, Mayo acquired its first station – Mid West Radio. The body responsible for adult and vocational education in the county, Mayo Vocational Education Committee (VEC), saw an opportunity to promote adult education over the airwaves and approached the management of Mid West Radio with a view to them producing some programming around the topic of education. A positive response was received, and the VEC was asked to assist in the research and production of a weekly one-hour programme. The programme was very successful, and drew a wide range of listeners – teachers, parents and those who were just interested in education. Programmes included all aspects of education, from pre-school to adult and third-level, and featured many prominent experts in their fields. The programmes were also very beneficial to the VEC in promoting its courses throughout the county.

After a period of three years the project concluded and did not re-emerge until the advent of community radio in 1995 when the Independent Radio and Television Commission (IRTC, now the Broadcasting Commission of Ireland, BCI) invited local communities throughout the country to apply for broadcasting licences. Mayo VEC, through its adult education service, had, as already mentioned, experience of producing and presenting educational broadcasting on the local commercial station – Mid West Radio – and was anxious to become involved again, this time with the community project. The Adult Education Board of the VEC initiated a process where it brought together a range of voluntary organisations and statutory groups, such as the county council, the town council and the VEC, to process an application for a licence. The Mayo Adult Education Board was of the view that the community service offered a more diverse range of opportunities for programmes for education, due to the very nature of its ethos, which in a sense complimented that of the Adult Education Board.

The participative process, which is the ethos of community radio, was in itself complementary to the work being promoted by the Adult Education Board. It was felt, too, that community radio had more scope to focus on topics and issues, which, in many cases, might only be of a minority interest, but yet important to the listeners involved. For example, the work done in adult literacy, which will be dealt with in more detail later in this chapter, proved to be of considerable significance and was later developed into a major national, radio and TV series – *Read, Write, Now* – and was broadcast on the public service broadcaster, RTÉ and other stations with ongoing back up from individual tutors and comprehensive supporting learning material.

The series commenced with the radio project in 1999 when the National Adult Literacy Agency, NALA, joined with a local commercial station in Tipperary, Tipp Fm, to broadcast a set of programmes aimed at supporting people with basic literacy skills. In Co. Mayo the VEC devised and produced a similar project. The IRTC, which was the national body responsible for independent broadcasting at the time, also supported the project. NALA developed a set of learning materials which were used by the listeners in conjunction with the programmes. A free-phone telephone line was also put in place to deal with enquiries. Following the success of the radio project, it was decided to develop the TV Series which involved the national broadcaster RTÉ delivering twelve half-hour weekly programmes, again supported by learning materials developed by NALA and in co-operation with the VECs throughout the country. *Read, Write, Now* was broadcast each year between 2000 and 2004 and at its peak attracted 270,000 viewers.

NALA continued to work with the Community Radio Forum and the local VECs and a radio version *of Read, Write, Now* was broadcast on a number of community stations including CRC Fm, Mayo; ICR, Donegal; NEAR Fm, Dublin; and RCB, Clare.

Following the granting of a licence to Community Radio Castlebar (CRC Fm), the Mayo VEC Adult Education Board, continued to support its development, and was actively involved in promoting educational broadcasting from the station. CRC Fm has also provided valuable opportunities for people involved in VEC courses to gain experience in broadcasting over the past 10 years and as a result, a number of former students now work as staff in the station and others have moved on to careers in broadcasting. Involvement in the skills of broadcasting has also been an important developmental process for many volunteers from the community, enabling them to gain a range of personal skills which can be transferred into their everyday lives.

Literacy through the Airwaves was proposed as a distant education radio project. Its purpose was to support adult literacy students in acquiring help with their reading and writing in their own homes, through the medium of radio. This particular approach to assisting students was thought to be especially significant in that it had many advantages over the formal student/tutor situation.

A major problem for people with reading and writing difficulties is to admit to others that they have this problem, and to seek help. For many years, and to some extent even today, people in the community generally find it hard to understand that individuals can go through the primary and post-primary school system, and yet still be unable to read and write. There is also an element of a stigma attached to people with learning difficulties, and thus the whole area has to be treated with the utmost sensitivity, with support given in a very confidential manner. Radio lends itself to this approach in that it allows contact with the student in a totally confidential setting. It is not even necessary for the tutor to know who the students are, except where the student requires individual support outside the radio programme.

In addition, because in many circumstances literacy tuition has to be delivered on a one-to-one basis, it is very demanding on tutor resources, and can limit the amount of provision available. Radio, however, allows an almost unlimited number of students to avail of tuition. Yet there is only need for one tutor – the programme presenter. Radio programmes supported with materials and audiotapes allow the students to set their own pace with learning, and they can repeat learning sessions as often as they like, as well as listening to the broadcast material. There has been much debate throughout the educational world about the efficacy of learning over the airwaves compared to the more traditional approaches, and it is not the intention of this article to deal with this topic. Suffice it to say that distance learning has been with us many years, ever since the 1960s when the Open University was first established. Increasingly also, media such as information technology is being used to maximise the delivery of learning.

The *Literacy through the Airwaves* project, developed by Mayo VEC, was not particularly unique, but perhaps it was innovative. In the initial project much thought was given to whether the thrust should be towards increased awareness or more specific learning – the latter was the direction chosen, even though it was felt that the audience for the programme would be very targeted – mainly adult literacy students. This would be somewhat different to the approach taken with the RTÉ series *Read, Write, Now* which initially concentrated on creating awareness, but also on identifying some basic learning points.

The Literacy through the Airwaves project was first initiated by NALA, who approached the Department of Education for funding to develop a series of programmes in co-operation with Tipp Fm. NALA was to produce the materials and the content of the programmes, while Tipp Fm were to provide the broadcasting facilities. The Adult Literacy scheme in South Tipperary operated under the auspices of South Tipperary VEC, which was also involved in the project by assisting students with follow up support. A project evaluation report, commissioned by NALA, set out the aims of the project as being:

> to design, produce and deliver a distance learning programme in adult basic education consisting of a series of radio programmes supported by a printed study pack which will help adults to improve their reading and writing skills (McSkeanne, 1999).

At the time NALA was developing the project with Tipp Fm, Mayo VEC's Adult Education Board were already working with CRC Fm on a similar project. The difference in Mayo, however, was that the lead role was taken by the VEC, and it was they who had applied separately to the Department of Education for funding for the project and then approached CRC Fm to seek their co-operation. On receipt of the funding, it was proposed to develop a series of twelve programmes based on literacy tuition sessions which could be broadcast once a week over a three-month period. Each programme involved a tutor and a student working their way through some of the learning materials. These materials were those developed by NALA and, as mentioned above, were in the form of a study pack. Packs were distributed to students as they registered for the course. The approach was that each programme would be broadcast once a week for one hour with a repeat broadcast later in the week. A student had volunteered to work with the presenter/tutor in studio and the listeners, effectively, eavesdropped and followed the programme in their own homes. The programmes were based on the material designed by

NALA so that listeners could follow with their study packs. In all, 35 students registered for the series. CRC Fm provided all the technical support and programmes were recorded on mini disc, and subsequently broadcast at the scheduled times. In order to support students who might have queries or required additional information, a special confidential help line was set up in the VEC, and listeners could call the Adult Literacy Organiser the morning after the programme. This line was well used by the students and the Adult Literacy Organiser dealt with a substantial range of calls. An interesting situation which derived from the calls was that many students requested tapes of the programme because they either wanted to do further study or because they had missed the programme in that particular week. The demand for tapes was such that the VEC commissioned a local supplier to produce a thousand sets, and long after the programme had finished re-quests were still being received for both the study pack and tapes.

The series has been repeated on an annual basis since 1999 when it was first broadcast, and is now considered to be part of the provision offered in adult literacy by Mayo VEC. An evaluation report of the project revealed some interesting findings in relation to the participants, as set out below.

Sex	Age Groups	Education Levels	Age Leaving School	Employment Status
Male = 51% Female = 49%	21-40 yrs = 51% 41-55 yrs = 40% Over 55 yrs = 6% Under 20 yrs = 3%	No qualifica-tions = 54% Group Cert = 29% Inter Cert = 14% Leaving Cert = 3%	Under 14 = 69% Between 14–15 = 29% Over 15 = 21%	Full-time = 28% Part-time = 28% At Home = 26% Unemployed = 9% Unspecified = 9%

(McSkeanne, 1999).

One of the aims of the project was to encourage people to come forward for help if they had reading and writing problems, and although this was not specifically quantified, there was some anecdotal evidence that a number of the students who came to the literacy centre for help had heard the radio programme.

The evaluation also sought feedback from students on the series, and generally the comments were positive. For example, one student said, "It opened up areas to me like the dictionary; the fables and poems were good". All of the students said they would follow a similar series again, as one person put it, "Definitely, I have already told my sister about it". A number of students also mentioned the encouragement the programme gave them to do something positive about their literacy problems. For example, one said, "It would give you the encouragement to go ahead into a centre". Another said, "I think it's a very good idea. You are at home and you can follow it there" and a third explained, "It makes you feel good to know that you are doing something" (McSkeanne, 1999).

The whole process of developing literacy through the airwaves was commented on by the evaluator, who said:

> The pilot phase of *Literacy through the Airwaves* has demonstrated that this developmental strategy in principle is possible at least on a small scale. It is an approach which is very familiar in Adult Education in the Adult Literacy sector. (McSkeanne, 1999: 39).

Mayo VEC has found the experience of working with CRC Fm very beneficial in the delivery of literacy provision to those learners who do not avail of the more formal system. These are the learners who are often the most educationally disadvantaged and radio is an effective method allowing them to study in a very confidential and independent way. CRC Fm is therefore fulfilling an important role in assisting the VEC to carry out its community education remit and is consequently also contributing to overall community development by its involvement in the education process.

Following the success of the *Literacy through the Airwaves* project a similar approach was taken to a series of programmes on the Irish language. Here the aim was to develop conversational Irish at an introductory level. A one-hour programme again was developed to run over some twelve weeks. The presenter, Padraig Lavin, who also produced the programme, did not have a student in the studio, unlike the literacy programme, but treated the listeners as his class. He also had a personal website and notes for each programme were posted on the site so that listeners could access them in their own time. While there was no formal evaluation done on this project, the anecdotal evidence was that it too had a significant listenership. In reviewing the project the VEC intend, at some time in the future, to examine the potential of using its own website in developing material to support further initiatives in broadcasting with CRC Fm.

A lot of what goes on in community radio fits in very well with the ethos of adult education, with many areas where there is common ground. For example, a key issue in adult education is participation, as it is in community radio. Community radio in Castlebar is concerned with development, both of the individual and of the community. So too is adult education. Community radio can be an effective educational tool as was illustrated by the *Literacy through the Airwaves* project. Access to education in a county like Mayo, which is rural in nature and geographically widespread with a dispersed population, presents an interesting challenge, and one that the medium of radio can meet in some respects. Community radio has the potential to enable people to access a range of education provision, but this requires innovative thinking and, of course, resources.

9

An Ghaeilge agus an Raidió Pobail: The Irish Language and Community Radio

Lisa Ní Choisdealbha

I mí Iúil na bliana 2002 cuireadh tús le tionscnamh úr nua. Ceapadh Comhordnaitheoir Gaeilge chun an Ghaeilge a chur chun cinn laistigh de na stáisiúin raidió neamhspleácha, idir cinn pobail agus cinn tráchtála. Scéim trí bliana a bhí ann agus déanann an caibidil seo cur síos ar an dul chun cinn a deineadh agus ar an tionchar a bhí ag an gComhordnaitheoir Gaeilge ar úsáid na Gaeilge sna stáisiúin pobail.

In July 2002 an Irish Language Co-ordinator was appointed by the Broadcasting Commission of Ireland (BCI). The appointment was the result of much discussion and debate which had taken place since 1999 when Bord na Gaeilge (now Foras na Gaeilge) and the then Independent Radio and Televeision Commission (IRTC, now the BCI) joined forces in an attempt to improve the position of the Irish language in independent radio stations in Ireland. An Irish Language Advisory Committee was established and its remit was to examine the types and level of use of Irish language programming in the independent sector, to identify factors that inhibit and support the production of Irish language programming and to make recommendations to encourage more Irish language usage on-air by independent radio and television stations.

From the very beginning, community radio had a strong voice in the development of Irish language policy with two representatives sitting on the committee, Fionnuala Mac Aodha, of Raidió na Life, and Rosemary Day, of Wired FM, who pushed hard for the appointment of a full-time Irish Language Development Officer. The publication of the Advisory Committee's *Irish Language Broadcasting in the Independent Broadcasting Sector* policy document in 2001 (IRTC, 2001) was the springboard for many of the Irish language developments and initiatives that have taken place in the years since. Included in the report were the IRTC's policy statement on Irish language programming, results of a survey on the status of Irish language programming on independent radio stations and a list of recommendations and appropriate actions to improve the position of the language. One such recommendation was the appointment of a person to coordinate the implementation of the recommendations. This appointment needed to be implemented in order for the successful completion of the remainder of the Committee's recommendations. A three-year contract for an Irish language co-ordinator was advertised and I got the job.

As with any job, it is vital to know what your starting position is before you can begin to improve it. The information available within the BCI regarding Irish language content on independent radio stations was poor. Commercial radio stations had to submit programme schedules, and any proposed changes to same, which resulted in some information, but this was limited. The same did not apply to community radio stations and therefore the first objective of the Irish Language Co-ordinator was to gather information. The information gathered from this survey would form the basis of the Co-ordinator's workplan and so it was important to know the amount of Irish language programming currently being broadcast; the programme areas where stations would like to de-

velop an Irish language dimension; Irish language training requirements; the reaction of listeners to Irish language programmes; the
awareness of Irish language organisations in the station's community; and the assistance that stations felt the Irish Language Co-
ordinator could give to them.

The results that emerged from the survey were slightly disappointing. The majority of community radio stations were broadcasting Irish language programmes, however there were few attempts made to involve the community in these programmes.
There was very little understanding of, or interaction between,
community radio stations and local Irish language organisations,
with quite a high number of stations unaware of the existence of
any Irish language organisations in their areas. This was surprising
considering many respondents stated that they would like more
interaction with local Irish language groups such as Gaelscoileanna
and Comhaltas Ceoltoirí Éireann. There was a strong sense from
the stations that the production of Irish language programmes
was a chore and this feeling was evident in the programmes themselves. Stations requested methods for making Irish programmes
more enjoyable for both the volunteers and the listeners. They
wanted ideas for Irish programmes that were upbeat, modern and
lively, moving away from the teacher approach to the language
and designing Irish programmes suitable for young people.

There was also a strong training element to the responses. All
stations recognised the need for Irish language training, not only
for those directly involved in Irish language programmes but also
to cater for volunteers who would like to learn Irish; presenters
of English programmes who would like to include small pieces of
Irish in their programmes; the development of Irish language programming ideas; Irish language presenters who would like to improve their level of Irish; and Irish speakers who would like an
opportunity to practise their spoken Irish. Not surprisingly, there
were quite a few references to sourcing funding for Irish language
programmes and also some requests for assistance in sourcing

presenters with Irish language skills. A sense of fear with regards to Irish language programming was strong in the responses to the survey. This is not something that was particular to the community sector – if anything, the fear of Irish language programming and its development was much stronger among commercial stations than it was among the community stations. Eliminating this fear was an issue that had to be dealt with, as Irish language programming would never be developed to its full potential within the community sector if the volunteers and management of the stations could not approach it in a positive manner. The results of the survey, coupled with the advice of the Irish Language Advisory Committee, in particular the community radio representatives on the Committee, resulted in the introduction of a number of Irish language initiatives for the community radio sector as described below.

Community stations, through their survey responses, declared an interest in improving the capabilities of their volunteers in spoken Irish, in particular, presenters of English programmes who wanted to use *cúpla focal* at various stages in the programme, for example in introductions and at advertisement breaks. The attention of the Irish Language Co-ordinator was constantly drawn to *Nathanna Cainte don Raidió* (IRTC, 2000), a booklet of simple Irish phrases suitable for use on radio, which had been produced and distributed by the Irish Language Advisory Committee in 2000. However, the single criticism of the booklet was the lack of assistance it gave with pronunciation. In an attempt to, firstly, make it easier for volunteers to learn Irish phrases, and secondly, make learning Irish more modern, *Nathanna Cainte don Raidió* was updated, improved and expanded and distributed to all community radio stations. The booklet was accompanied by an interactive CD-Rom (BCI, 2003), giving volunteers the opportunity to hear the phrases spoken in a choice of three dialects. The aim of this was to give presenters the confidence to use the phrases by listening to them being spoken. Reaction to both the booklet and

CD-Rom was extremely positive, not only among radio stations but also among schools and community groups.

Station specific ID's and programme promos were recorded for each community radio station in Irish. This was done to avoid the Irish language being given one weekly slot on-air and only being heard at that particular time each week. Irish language jingles were also recorded and distributed for special occasions such as St. Patrick's Day and Christmas. These ensured that each station would be broadcasting some amount of Irish each day, regardless of how small the amount. It also assisted in the task of trying to make the regular broadcasting of Irish more acceptable.

Glór na nGael is an organisation which aims to develop the viability and durability of the Irish language in Ireland by means of a community competition in which partnership with local groups is central. It is pursued through the recognition and coordination of the resources and skills of each community. For some years now the BCI has been sponsoring two prizes in the national Glór na nGael competition. In previous years there had been one prize for the radio station which made the most effective use of Irish and another prize for the Glór na nGael committee which worked best with the local radio station, be it community or commercial. In 2002, the competition was changed so that one prize now goes to a community station and one prize to a commercial station for the best use of Irish. In the case of community radio stations, this involved Irish used on-air, among station volunteers and also in the local community. Previous winners include Wired Fm for the Wired Luimnigh project, which drew the Irish speaking community of Limerick city together with the ultimate aim of broadcasting entirely through Irish during the weekend. Cork Campus Radio also won for its large and diverse range of Irish language programmes, offering both students and local Irish language organisations the opportunity to broadcast in Irish to the college campus and also to the wider city region. Both of these stations have provided local Irish language organisations with an outlet for the language, resulting in increased motivation and a new lease of life among the members of the Irish language organisations.

Affording members of the community access to the airwaves is one of the key aims of community radio and this was fully exploited to the benefit of Irish language broadcasting through the Scéim na Scoile project. It strengthened connections between community stations and local Irish language groups and organisations, as was requested by the stations in their survey responses. This project gives primary and secondary school pupils the opportunity to record an Irish language programme, which is then broadcast by the community radio station in their area. There are currently more than 50 schools involved in this project, broadcasting on 13 radio stations. This not only increases the Irish language output of the participating stations but it also builds strong ties between the community radio station and the schools and young people in the community.

The BCI and the Irish Language Advisory Committee have always recognised that there is more to Irish language development in radio stations than programming. The Irish language strand of the old New Adventures in Broadcasting scheme promoted the production of Irish language programmes in radio stations. However, it was also understood that there is a need to look at more long-term improvements that would benefit the development of the language within the station, and that individual radio stations should have the opportunity to develop the use of the language within their stations, as they see fit. To facilitate this, a fund was established which offered community stations the opportunity to plan for the long-term improvement of Irish within their own station. Various initiatives were undertaken, ranging from the purchase of equipment for Irish language organisations to use, to Irish language classes for volunteers, to the hiring of a co-ordinator to encourage more Irish language organisations to participate in programmes. As a result of the Community Radio Irish Language Fund, Raidió Pobal Inis Eoghain launched a booklet and accompanying CD of myths and legends from the Inishowen peninsula. This was distributed to all of the community stations in the country as well as being distributed widely throughout Inis Eoghain itself. Work has already begun on its translation into other European languages to cater for use on radio stations in other parts of Europe.

In 2003, Conradh na Gaeilge appointed Julian de Spáinn to organise and improve its annual Irish language festival, Seachtain na Gaeilge, throughout Ireland. As a result of meetings between the Seachtain na Gaeilge steering group and the BCI a series of workshops were organised in March each year. These workshops were for primary and secondary school pupils to teach them how to put a radio programme together. It also gave them the opportunity to record their programmes and to gain an understanding of how a studio works. For the most part, these workshops were hosted by community radio stations, allowing the stations to reach pupils and teachers in their localities with an interest in Irish. Combined with the Scéim na Scoile initiative, they laid the foundation for developing stronger relationships between the stations and the schools, resulting in more schools producing programmes in Irish for community radio stations after the week was over.

Training in the Irish language was not available to community radio volunteers prior to the appointment of the Irish Language Co-ordinator. Since 2002 an Irish language workshop has been included in the programme of the Community Radio Training Féile each year. This workshop has always been well attended and well received by the volunteers. A training weekend for volunteers already involved in Irish language programming was held in Limerick city in September 2004. Training weekends such as this have given volunteers access to and training from Irish language broadcasters, not only from within the community radio sector but also from independent commercial radio, RTÉ Raidió na Gaeltachta, TG4 and RTÉ. These weekends also encouraged networking between the various community stations allowing for the sharing and development of programming ideas.

In January 2005 a meeting was held for station managers in order to gain an understanding of how they would like to see the Irish language developed in the sector. At this meeting it was pointed out that volunteers not involved in Irish language programmes should be given an opportunity to learn and improve their spoken Irish. It was felt that this would increase the acceptance of the language within the station. The first such training weekend for both Irish and non-Irish speakers was held in Westport, Co. Mayo in February 2005 and it was a resounding success. Two strands of workshops ran simultaneously, one focusing on Irish language presentation skills and the other on conversational Irish. The weekend dispelled a lot of fears regarding the speaking and learning of Irish. It allowed station staff to see the language used in an enjoyable and relevant way.

Employees from Irish language organisations such as Foras na Gaeilge, Conradh na Gaeilge and Glór na nGael were invited to speak to and meet with the community station volunteers in an attempt to broaden the Irish language contact base for each station, both locally and nationally. It has also opened up a new funding opportunity for community stations with organisations such as Foras na Gaeilge offering funding schemes for the promotion and development of Irish in the community.

Irish language radio training is taking a more formalised approach with the beginning of a part-time Higher Diploma in Radio Skills. This distance education course is being run by Acadamh na hOllscolaíochta Gaeilge in Áras Mháirtín Uí Chadhain, An Cheathrú Rua, Co. Galway, an outreach of NUI Galway. A similar course is planned by Ballyfermot College of Further Education in Dublin. Such developments are proof of the increased interest in Irish language broadcasting and should have a positive effect on the amount of Irish programmes broadcast by community radio stations in the future.

Community radio stations have placed huge importance on the development of the Irish language, both on the air and also among volunteers. This became evident with the formation of an Irish language sub-group within CRAOL (see Chapter 4), and also with the appointment and inclusion of an Irish Language Officer on CRAOL's executive committee.

As well as organising Irish language initiatives that are suitable and open to all community stations, the Irish Language Advisory Committee has given its support to specific projects from individual community stations. These include Wired Fm, Cork Campus Radio and Ros Fm. The board of Wired Fm realised that there was a large number of Irish speakers in Limerick city who did not know each other and who did not have an outlet for using their Irish. Given that Wired Fm did not broadcast during the weekend, they decided to use their spare broadcasting time to unite the Irish speakers of the city. From this, Wired Luimnigh was born. Following a public meeting to gauge the level of interest and number of potential volunteers, training sessions were organised and Wired Luimnigh began its pilot broadcast in May 2003. The pilot project was extremely successful and the reaction from the volunteers was so positive that it was decided to continue Wired Luimnigh in September. Since then Wired Luimnigh has gone from strength to strength increasing its broadcasting hours, its volunteer base and its range of programmes. It caters for listeners of every taste and age with programmes teaching Irish to parents whose children are attending the Gaelscoileanna in the city, to programmes for those with an interest in bluegrass music. It was also the winner of the New Adventures in Broadcasting Irish programme strand in 2005 with *Fonn na Seachtaine,* a 12 part interactive programme teaching traditional Irish music through Irish over the airwaves and internet. The BCI published a training handbook for use in other community radio stations who wish to increase their Irish language service. Called *An Droichead,* which means bridge, it emphasises the need to build the community of Irish speakers and learners through the radio project (Day, 2007).

Cork Campus Radio also welcomed its first non-student group into the station in 2003. Gael Taca is an Irish language organisation whose aim is to make the Irish language more visible to the people of Cork city and county. The organisation, through the FÁS Community Employment (CE) scheme, has five employees. Cork Campus Radio provided radio training for Gael Taca and before long they were broadcasting weekly, hour-long Irish language programmes. Since then, the programme has become a regular weekly feature on CRY, Youghal, on Cork University Hospital Radio and on Clonmel Hospital Radio in Tipperary. The opportunity to broadcast has given new life to Gael Taca. Not only has it increased the personal skills of its participants but it has allowed them to reach a wider group of people through the airwaves and also to attend Irish language training weekends and the Community Radio Training Féile (see Chapter 4).

In order to increase the Irish used by volunteers on Ros FM and the involvement of members of the community with an interest in Irish, Ros FM investigated the possibility of appointing an Irish Language Officer. The main element of the project was the recruitment of a part-time Irish Language Officer who would focus on developing and expanding the range of Irish language programmes currently broadcast by the station, aiming for the delivery of a high-quality product; incorporating the wider use of Irish in the overall schedule in terms of vox-pops, greetings and dedications, programme introductions and exits; promoting and developing an Irish language culture through the use of dual signage and general conversation through Irish within the station; and establishing links with groups involved in the promotion of the Irish language, both locally and nationally, in an attempt to increase the level of involvement in Irish language programmes.

Ros FM adopted a partnership approach to this initiative, involving the station itself, the BCI's Irish Language Co-ordinator and the Irish Language Officer of Roscommon County Council.

This was the first time that such a partnership has been used for the development of the language in a community radio station.

So what does the future hold for the development of the Irish language in the community radio sector? There were a lot of positive developments in Irish language broadcasting on community radio stations in the three years of the project. Despite this, changes to work practices must take place in the not-too-distant future. A recent review and evaluation of the work and effectiveness of the Irish Language Advisory Committee completed by Polaris HR stated that radio stations in general must become more involved in Irish language planning for the future. It also highlighted the need for all stations to take more ownership of Irish language initiatives and projects which are currently up and running and to adopt a more strategic and long-term approach to Irish language development in the future. To achieve this some changes are being implemented. It was recommended that the title of the Irish Language Advisory Committee be changed to Irish Language Development Committee. This is to reflect the fact that the committee has been focusing on the development of Irish language broadcasting since its inception.

The BCI was conscious that the committee structure and membership should reflect its partnership approach by ensuring that each interest group is adequately represented on the committee. CRAOL therefore nominates two representatives to represent the interests of the community radio sector. These representatives are responsible for ensuring that the interests of the community radio sector are discussed at committee meetings; updating the sector with any relevant information; encouraging the sector to support initiatives recommended by the committee; and co-ordinating the activities of the sector in the execution of the committee's initiatives. These changes were made to achieve two things. The first is that the initiatives planned by the committee will be as a result of direct involvement and instruction from the community sector. The second is that the capacity for developing and implementing Irish language initiatives will be increased as the sector becomes more involved in the planning and implementation of initiatives. Community stations have already started to focus on this method of working, as is evident from the appointment by CRAOL of an Irish Language Officer and the formation of an Irish language sub-group. These ensure that community radio stations have a greater sense of ownership of Irish language development within their sector.

There was consistent praise by community radio stations for the work done by both the Irish Language Advisory Committee and the Irish Language Co-ordinator over the course of the three-year project. Every effort was made by the Committee and the Co-ordinator to ensure that each Irish language initiative or project was user-friendly, modern, upbeat and, most importantly, relevant to the stations using it. To this end, the involvement of stations at every stage from product development to evaluation was of the utmost importance. The end result of this partnership approach has been a greater sense of ownership of the Irish language initiatives and products, a heightened sense of enthusiasm about them and a willingness to use them as much as possible.

"Tús maith leath na hoibre" a deirtear agus cinnte tá sé sin fíor go mór mór ó thaobh cur chun cinn na Gaeilge sna stáisiúin raidió pobail. Níl aon dabht ach gur éirigh leis an tionscnamh seo mar gheall ar an tacaíocht, an meon dearfach agus an cúnamh a tháinig ó lucht na stáisiúin pobail. Is ionann comhairle maith agus cúnamh agus bhí an t-ádh dearg leis an gComhordnaitheoir Gaeilge mar bhí idir comhairle maith agus cúnamh ann i gcónaí ó na stáisiúin pobail. Ón tús bhí gaol iontach idir an Coiste Comhairleach um Chláracha Gaeilge, an Comhordaitheoir Gaeilge agus na stáisiúin pobail. Níor tháinig ach feabhas ar an ngaol seo le linn na trí bliana agus tá na torthaí le feiscint san obair atá déanta agus sa mhéadú a tháinig, ní amháin ar líon na gclaracha Gaeilge atá á chraoladh ach freisin ar an athrú meoin maidir leis an nGaeilge atá soiléir sna stáisiúin pobail ó shin.

10

Student Community Radio

Catríona Chambers

Since its inaugural broadcast on 31 July 1995, Cork Campus Radio 97.4 Fm has developed and maintained a unique programme schedule, catering for a diversity of needs and interests reflecting student and community issues and concerns. The station produces a 60 per cent speech to 40 per cent music weekly broadcast output throughout Cork city and its environs, from purpose-built studios at Áras na MacLéinn, UCC, from 8.00 am to 5.30 pm Monday to Friday, 50 weeks of the year, in accordance with the licence granted by the Broadcasting Commission of Ireland (BCI). The station broadcasts on campus, in the multi-functional Devere Hall, in shops in Áras na MacLéinn, to a 30-mile radius around the city of Cork and via the internet (www.ucc.ie/ccr) to the world.

Aiming to promote balanced student and community programming, the station encourages access to and involvement in radio for individuals and groups to present their ideas and views. It provides a medium for educational programming and an active community relations programme, offering itself both as a valuable resource tool and as a facilitator for Cork community projects, encouraging access to programming and participation from the wider community of Cork and, of course, it provides a medium of expression for the student population. Representatives of the college's academic staff have also been involved with the station, either as guests, or as programme presenters, over the past decade.

Staffed by a full-time manager, Catríona Chambers, a full-time producer/technician, Kieran Hurley, and over 90 student and community volunteers, Cork Campus Radio operates under the principles of the AMARC Europe Community Radio Charter (see appendix). It is a not-for-profit community of interest broadcaster. Every emphasis is placed on the student volunteers adopting a professional attitude to their work. This is reinforced by facilitating training workshops, and volunteers are afforded the opportunity to attend events such as the annual Community Radio Training Féile (see Chapter 4). Around 1,000 volunteers have passed through the station over the past decade, with many progressing to full-time media careers.

Cork Campus Radio has long provided excellent practical training and experience of live broadcasting to in-house and visiting personnel. Media students from other third level colleges in the city, such as Coláiste Stiofán Naofa and St. John's College, often spend time on work experience at the station, and training is also offered to groups such as the Northside Folklore Project (NFP) and Gael Taca in broadcasting-related issues – the latter producing a weekly series entitled *Clár Gael Taca* every Thursday 4.00–5.00 pm (see Chapter 9). The NFP is currently producing *How's it Goin' Boy?*, a weekly series exploring the cultures of Cork. The station provides nearly 50 hours of programming per week with all output researched, produced and presented to as professional a standard as possible, adopting a balance between the student sound and public service broadcasting ideals.

The station contributes to media diversity in the Cork city area, providing access for a wide range of groups within the community, particularly minorities, and those under-represented in public service and commercial media. For example, Cork Campus Radio produced a six-part series documenting life in Cork Prison, the men's committal jail on Rathmore Road. Produced and recorded by

Chambers and Hurley, the series, entitled *A Life without Liberty*, won the Law Society of Ireland's Justice Media Award 2004, and was short-listed for an ESB National Media Award. In association with a national campaign, Know Racism, the station produced a multicultural/anti-racism series entitled *Diversity Speaks*. This featured participants from Iraqi Kurdistan, Cork Travellers' Visibility Group, Turkey, Cameroon, Pakistan and Ukraine. The series was short-listed for the MAMA Awards 2004, and has remained on the schedule since. More recently, the station was presented with a Glór na nGael Award for its consistent promotion of the Irish language, and two student volunteers reached the shortlist of this year's Oxygen Student Media Awards.

Cork Campus Radio also produces a weekly series for the Lesbian, Gay, Bisexual and Transexual (LGBT) community of Cork, *Pink Parade,* and has also generated a number of Cork-themed socio-documentaries including *Jews in Cork; The English Market* and *The Cork Arts Theatre*. Cork Campus Radio has long been associated with the arts, and this is represented by programmes devoted to film, theatre and literature. The station also produces a weekly health and well-being show, Irish Language programming, current affairs, sport, science, comedy, and a number of music shows, with new programming ideas from volunteers and listeners always welcome. Current and forthcoming projects include documentaries on substance abuse and young people in Cork; the legacy of the Huguenots in Cork, *Cork Anthologies*; and a series for, and presented by, students with disabilities. The station also exchanges students with Queen's Radio in Queen's University, Belfast.

Maintaining a strong relationship between UCC and the wider community of Cork is paramount. Consequently, the station has been involved with local annual events such as InterMedia and the Woodford Bourne Cork Midsummer Festival and produced programming in conjunction with Cork 2005, the European Cultural Capital experience. The station facilitates a programme slot for UCC Students' Union, *S.U. Weekly,* which has proved a popular addition to the schedule. As well as that, together with John Smith & Son Bookshop, a book club was created. According to Chambers:

> This idea has really taken off. The book club meets on the first Thursday of every month, encouraging a wide variety of staff and students to participate, with new faces popping up each month. It has helped foster a strong relationship between Áras na MacLéinn and UCC, and we look forward to another successful season.

In 1995, Cork Campus Radio formed part of a group of 11 stations involved in the Community Radio Pilot Project (see Chapter 3). Full licences were subsequently granted by the Independent Radio and Television Commission (IRTC, forerunner of the BCI) on successful completion of the trial period. The oldest student radio station in Ireland (Wired Fm in Limerick and Flirt Fm in Galway followed just weeks later), Cork Campus Radio continues to serve UCC and the community of Cork. As Chambers says:

> While we have maintained strong links with a number of communities in Cork, the station could further develop its relationship with UCC – I would encourage academic and administrative staff to participate in programming, either as guests or presenters. They are more than welcome – the door is always open!

The origins of Flirt Fm can be traced back to the early 1990s. The Students' Union had been operating Rag Week Radio for a number of years and, in 1993, the Radio Society was formed with the aim of setting up a full time station in what was then University College Galway but became the National University of Ireland, Galway or NUI, Galway.

When the IRTC invited groups to apply to operate a community of interest station as part of its pilot project in community radio, the Radio Society Auditor, Andrew O'Baoill, approached Seán Mac Íomhair, Director of Audio-Visual Services in UCG, who had previously signed the licence contracts for Rag Week

stations on behalf of the college. He directed O'Baoill to Gearóid
Ó Tuathaigh, Vice-President for Development and External Affairs, who enlisted college support and the co-operation of Gay
Corr, Director of the Regional Technical College (Galway RTC,
now the Galway Mayo Institute of Technology, GMIT). Together
they prepared the application which, following a public hearing in
October 1994, was successful in gaining what turned out to be
one of four contracts for student radio stations. Flirt Fm was officially launched on 28 September 1995, by the Minister for the
Arts, Culture and the Gaeltacht, Michael D. Higgins. The name is
not an acronym though it is often mistaken for one.

The station initially began life in the old Audio-Visual Department on the UCG Concourse. This was a stop-gap measure due
to a delay in the completion of the purpose-built studio. Unfortunately, this led to restricted broadcast hours, with the station
only on air for two hours a day. This was steadily expanded upon,
however, and finally the station moved to its new studios in the
old IMI Warehouse on 22 November 1995, exactly one year to
the day after the IRTC informed the company that a licence was
to be granted. The new station rapidly captured the interest of
students on both sides of the city. College societies such as An
Cummann Craic, the Political Discussion Society and PLUTO
produced some of the station's finest programmes in its earliest
years. Flirt Fm rapidly earned a reputation as a home to new, alternative and old, but often ignored, music in Galway. At a time
when commercial radio was driving a middle of the road course,
bands such as the Smiths, Joy Division, and the Pixies found a new
lease of life amongst the student community in Galway. In its first
year of broadcasting, over 250 students from UCG and the RTC
were involved in all aspects of programming and station administration. In its second year, the station expanded its schedule,
broadcasting 12 hours each weekday. Weekend broadcasts ensured that the station truly provided a unique and all encompassing service for the student and youth populations of Galway.

Flirt Fm received funding for 18 months initially from both institutions. It received an extra £5,000 in 1997 when the licence was extended for one year beyond the pilot stage. That year, following two referenda, funding was secured from student capitation revenue, thus securing the station's financial viability. Initial teething problems tested the mettle of the student crew. The IRTC noted that many of the station's problems were similar to those experienced by fellow third level operations in Cork and Limerick. Resources were always tight for campus radio, but the dedication of Flirt Fm's volunteers and the sheer determination of station manager O'Baoill meant they proved successful in the end. Stories of his immense dedication, enthusiasm and unusual methods are still talked about in the corridors of Flirt Fm – how he read chapters of books on air to keep up the talk content and how he spent overnights in the studio when there was no lock on the door. The initial pilot project provided the basis for a successful application for a new five-year licence which was granted by the IRTC in 1998.

By this time O'Baoill had returned to his studies and Fiona McNulty, a graduate of the RTC, took over as station manager. Under her guidance the station developed its service, broadcasting from mid-afternoon until late evening. Its flagship news and current affairs programme, *Teatime*, garnered much critical acclaim. Presented by Gavin Jennings, it resulted in some of the station's finest programming with particular focus on events in the North. Flirt Fm was the only campus station to broadcast live from Belfast during the North's assembly elections.

By 1999 things were changing fast in third level education in Galway. UCG morphed into NUI, Galway and the RTC became GMIT. Major restoration work commenced on the IMI Warehouse, soon to become Áras Uí Chathail, where the station's studios were based. This resulted in major disruption to the station despite the best efforts of the new manager, Yvonne Igoe. The traditional 24 hour broadcasts for Rag Week had to be cancelled due to the ongoing work. By the summer the station resembled a building site, suffering flooding, a rodent invasion and the unique experience of the manager arriving at work to find the studio door bricked up. Her immense resilience and the dedication of the station's volunteers ensured that it survived the continual disruptions and entered the new millennium continuing to provide a unique service to the students of Galway. Igoe was succeeded by Keith Wallace, another manager in the front line of Flirt.

By 2001 the building work had been completed but sadly, for the station, a planned move back to the old Audio-Visual Department was cancelled, with the studio space allocated to the NUI, Galway Archaeology Department. In October 2001 Fiona Ní Lionnáin began her tenure as station manager. She oversaw a major overhaul of both the station's schedule and its broadcast facilities. Programmes were extended and, for the first time in a number of years, a Breakfast Show began. New radio documentaries were produced as well as brand new radio dramas. Programme teams were developed with each evening dedicated to a particular genre of music. Flirt Fm became the only station in Galway to dedicate an entire evening to Metal and Punk music as well as providing a unique access point for student DJs to gain valuable experience. During this time the studio and office were completely renovated, providing a professional feel to the station. Áine Lyne continued in this vein when she commenced her role as manager in 2003. The station produced a number of special programmes on Galway personalities as well as the Special Olympics. Through Áine's contributions, Flirt Fm became an active participant in CRAOL (see Chapter 4). September 2003 saw a major breakthrough for the station with the opening of a new studio in GMIT. Years in planning, with many false dawns, the studio finally helped GMIT students to feel like a real part of Flirt Fm.

Over the past ten years the station has won many awards with *An Cumann Craic* setting the trend early on. Possibly Flirt Fm's proudest moment came when President McAleese presented the station with a National Broadcasting Award for Equality in March

2000. The station also picked up a Smedia in 2004 for its documentary *Nomads*. Reflecting on the past, the next station manager Ross Cunningham is proud of what has been achieved:

> Since the station came on air over 2,000 students have been involved in radio production. We have provided a voice for many marginalised groups in society and have brought student culture to the people of Galway. Flirt Fm has been a genuine alternative sound on the airways of the city.

Wired Fm was part of the original IRTC pilot project for community radio. Mary Immaculate College, University of Limerick (MIC) applied for a pilot project licence and the application was co-ordinated by Rosemary Day. The station was successful and began broadcasting for two hours a day in 1995. Today the station broadcasts nine hours a day, Monday to Thursday and broadcasts an Irish Language service for four hours on Fridays and Saturdays for the community of Irish speakers in the city. Initially, the University of Limerick (UL) and the Regional College of Technology (RTC, now the Limerick Institute of Technology, LIT) were equal partners in the campus radio venture. Today MIC and LIT are the partners in this very successful radio station.

Wired Fm broadcasts a youth-oriented and friendly service and its mission statement calls for it:

> To provide a service that entertains while at the same time provides an accessible platform for information, debate and concerns pertaining to all aspects of student life and to create an awareness of the student community in the region.

The station has two studios, one based in the Library building at MIC, the other based in the students' union centre in LIT. Over 120 students currently volunteer on a weekly basis for work in the station and form the backbone of Wired Fm.

The management structure is truly reflective of the community of interest that the station serves, with two staff members and two students, one from the Student Union and one from the Radio Society, representing each college on the board of directors. The station has engaged on a number of occasions in facilitated self-evaluations which have led to the design and implementation of new management structures. The station is now run through the board supported by a number of committees (promotion, funding and training) which strengthen the station within the college communities and ensure a real sense of ownership among the student body.

A recent survey of students on each of the campuses showed that the majority of students listened to the station and their former manager, Nessa McGann, describes their success as follows:

> If you ask a college student "What's so good about Wired Fm?", they will give reasons such as "it's good to hear our own voices", "it's great for training if you want to go into media", "they play real music you don't get on the other stations" and "I like hearing my friends make fools of themselves on the air"! If you ask a member of Wired Fm why they volunteer on the stations they will tell you that it helps to make new friends and to fit in somewhere in college. Many will say that it helps you to figure out if you want to get a job in the media.

Each year the station employs four students on paid, cooperative work placement as part of the BA in Media and Communications course in MIC. Of the students who have undertaken this work placement or volunteered with Wired FM, four are now working in local newspapers around the country, two are working full-time in community radio, four are working in national newspapers, seven are in local radio stations and five are in RTÉ television. Wired Fm has proven a fertile training ground for journalists and broadcasters since it first came on air.

Wired Fm is also proud of the interaction students have with members of their local community. Without the station they might never get to meet young people who have cerebral palsy, new immigrants and young people from the most disadvantaged parts of Limerick city. Wired Fm believes that it is important that students who have the privilege of a third level education get the opportunity to really work with and meet members of communities they might not otherwise encounter. This learning opportunity for students and for outside community groups is facilitated through specially-designed training courses and sessions and programme production. A programme run with the Limerick Youth Service enables young people who have dropped out of formal schooling to learn about the media, pick up sound engineering skills and spend some time on a university campus mentored by and socialising with those who stayed in the system. This has proven valuable to both sets of participants.

Half of the funding for the radio station comes from capitation grants from the students' unions. College staff give their expertise and experience free of charge and the rest of the budget is sourced through grant funding and sponsorship raised by the station manager. Grant aid for projects which Wired Fm believes are beneficial to the students and to the wider community are targeted, for example Development Education Aid, enabling the participation of people with disabilities in mainstream education and society, the promotion of the Irish language and health awareness.

Wired Fm has gone through many changes, some fundamental such as the ownership and management structures, some more superficial, such as name changes. Provisionally called RadioActive, names such as STAB Radio and RíRá were mooted before the students, with an eye to our increasingly techno futures, voted for Wired Fm. Each of these changes has been student-led – former managers (Sarah McDonald, Eoin Brady, Duncan O'Toole, Darren Connolly and Nessa McGann) facilitated and supported the students but student priorities take precedence always in Wired Fm. The students give the station its strength, vitality and originality. The station's first slogan captured this well when it described itself as "Wired, weird and wonderful!"

11

Support for Community Radio

Stephanie Comey and Margaret Tumelty

Funding is a perennial issue for all community and voluntary organisations and community radio is no different. Community
radio programming, training, evaluation methods and station
structures have evolved and developed over the years, so too
have the ideas, conversations, debates and perspectives on funding. A lot of experience and learning has accrued since 1994 and
the sharing of this information has facilitated the sector's ability to
respond to the ongoing challenge of funding. The funding environment is never static. New funding sources can become available while old reliable sources can disappear. This means that
there is no one solution to the challenge of funding, but rather a
need for a dynamic, adaptive and innovative approach – one that
is capable of responding to the changing funding environment
while remaining compatible with the ethos of community radio.
The development of the sector's capacity with regard to funding
has happened over time and through a lot of hard work. This section attempts to briefly outline how the principles which underpin
the sector's approach to funding have developed.

The origins of the current policy in relation to funding and
community radio can be traced back to the community radio pilot
project of 1995-1997 (see Chapter 3) when the regulatory body
(then IRTC, now BCI) licensed 11 community radio stations for

an 18-month period as a trial, or experiment, to test the viability of long-term community radio projects. There were a number of expectations of the stations involved in the pilot project. One of these was that stations should develop their funding strategies based on two key principles, namely, that funding would be obtained from a diversity of sources and that sponsorship would be locally sourced. The requirement for a diversity of sources has its origins in the AMARC Europe Charter (see appendix) as a guarantee of the independence of programming. Apart from the potential vulnerability of a station that is over-reliant on any one source of funding, such reliance also has the potential to impact on the editorial independence of a station's programming if the availability of that funding became contingent on a particular approach being taken to programming. The IRTC required that community radio stations source advertising and sponsorship from within their catchment areas, thus ensuring that they remained relevant to the local areas.

In the early days some within the sector believed that advertising would constitute a key source of revenue. This was based on an assumption that community radio would mimic a commercial radio funding model, based on advertising and sponsorship. This was encouraged by an initial willingness from advertisers to contribute to community radio, but also by the lack of any experience of an alternative funding model. Some stations targeted advertising and sponsorship and allocated staff resources to sourcing this type of funding. As time went on, however, it became apparent that advertising was not going to provide sufficient funds and that in many ways, the "cost" of sourcing this type of funding, in terms of commissions and staff/volunteer time, itself became prohibitive. The commercial radio funding model is dependent on the existence of audience figures and the tailoring of programming to attract maximum audience levels, which in turn attracts advertisers. Community radio is about a diversity of programming, alternative programming, programming that is made by and directed at the community in which the station is based. This does not equate with programming that is designed to maximise mainstream listenership. Yet, despite these differences, many stations pursued this approach. The experience of Irish community radio stations has been replicated across Europe, wherein advertising and sponsorship have failed to materialise as the great funding sources.

At the end of the pilot project, the Community Radio Policy which was formulated articulated the learning and conclusions reached in relation to funding. This became incorporated into the Community Radio Policy of the IRTC (1997) and later of the BCI (2002). The BCI's Community Radio Policy supports the view that community radio stations should be funded from a diversity of sources. The policy, as it relates to funding, has three main components. First, no more than 50 per cent of income can be secured from any one source. Second, a maximum of six minutes advertising/sponsorship is allowed per hour and stations may only broadcast advertisements which relate to work opportunities, events, businesses or services within the specific area. Third, the Commission will support efforts to increase the resources available to community broadcasters and specific initiatives will be considered.

In 2000, a special meeting of the Community Radio Forum was called to specifically review funding and to make recommendations in light of the Commission's own review of community radio funding. As a basis for the discussion, the IRTC prepared a funding profile based on audited accounts from stations for the year 1998. The profile showed that the total income for the sector in 1998 was €375,000. On-air commercial activity (advertising and sponsorship) accounted for 25 per cent of income. Off-air commercial activity accounted for 6 per cent of income while grant aid accounted for 48 per cent. Membership accounted for 12 per cent while fundraising accounted for 7 per cent.

A number of key points arose for discussion at that meeting. There was a recognition that community radio was in an ongoing process of financial development. There was also a recognition that in five years the sector had secured a funding basis comprised of a variety of funding sources and compatible with the ethos of community radio. There was a shift in emphasis over this time, away from an operational approach to funding, which existed by necessity in the early days, to a more strategic approach to funding. On-air commercial activity had not been as successful as first predicted – as discussed, raising advertising and sponsorship revenue was, of itself, labour intensive and involved an expenditure by the station. Attracting grant aid was, arguably, not as labour intensive as sourcing on-air commercial activity. There was more grant aid funding available than that available through advertising and sponsorship. In the first five years, grant aid had been received from a range of funders including LEADER, the Department of Social, Community and Family Affairs, a range of European funding initiatives, Bord na Gaeilge, the Higher Education Authority, Area Development Management, the National Social Services Board, a range of government departments and, of course, FÁS (the government agency that runs the Community Employment (CE) Scheme through which most of the staff of Irish community radio stations are employed). This raised the need for stations to be clearly recognised as strongly positioned within the community sector, in their ethos and the nature of their organisation.

Stations that had been successful in attracting large-scale grant aid, however, offered an interesting perspective. Stations had used their training function as a basis for grant aid. Despite the enthusiasm for this type of funding, some stations welcomed the funding but found the subsequent management and administration required in the running of a large-scale training project became a drain on their limited resources. Secondly, while grants provide a lucrative source of funding, they do, in the main, fund specific activities which must be undertaken by the station. For this reason they are not a source of income that can be guaranteed to fund core operating costs.

The experience of stations that had sought grant funding was that community radio was a new concept for many funders and there was considerable work to be done in positioning community radio within the community and voluntary sector rather than the media sector. The publication of the government's *White Paper on the Community and Voluntary Sector* saw a change in the levels of funding available for community and voluntary organisations. There was a need to increase awareness among key funders of what community radio was and of its position within this sector.

The experience of the pilot project highlighted the need to ensure that programming is determined primarily by the community served. This approach necessitates that the community served always takes some responsibility for supporting the operation of a community station in its area. The role of volunteers in relation to funding was discussed at meetings of the stations involved in the pilot project (see Chapters 3 and 4). It was generally agreed that volunteers need to appreciate that their involvement in community radio requires them to engage themselves in many aspects of its operation, including fundraising. Funding sources that are integrated into the programming and outreach activities of stations can be of greater relevance to volunteers. It was argued that grant aid for specific programming initiatives and for off-air commercial activity, such as training provision, has more relevance for volunteers than advertising and sponsorship. Volunteers may not believe that they have the expertise to source this type of funding. The contribution that volunteers and paid staff made was also discussed, particularly in terms of how this can be recognised and quantified, not least in acknowledging the in-kind contribution towards funding projects.

Much was learned over the first five years of broadcasting. One significant lesson revealed to community radio activists exactly what they meant by terming themselves "not-for-profit" enterprises. The sector's position in terms of commercial income became clarified as the provision of the means to operate and this is now a cornerstone of its ethos, particularly in terms of its own independence and the independence of its programming. In a review of community radio stations conducted by the BCI in 2003, stations reported that while funding was still an issue for them, and likely to continue to be one for the future, the majority of stations were financially stable by this time. There was also recognition that the sector needed to build its capacity in relation to funding and that a key element was the exchange of information and networking between stations. Another important element was the need for ethos promotion, that funding can not be viewed in isolation from the other activities within the station – that the programming ethos, training activities and station structures all contribute to the station's ethos which itself contributes to the station's eligibility to apply for grant aid. The other key points raised by that review were that the sector recognised that funding will be an ongoing issue for community radio stations as it is for all voluntary and community organizations; that the funding model for community stations is more akin to that of a community or voluntary organisation rather than the commercial funding model used in other areas of broadcasting; and that community radio stations were at various stages of financial development.

The funding sources and strategies in place in most stations were found to have been largely successful and the sector is now financially stable. Stations were receiving funding from a variety of sources which included on-air commercial activity, off-air commercial activity (rental of equipment/studio hire and training), grant aid, membership fees and community fundraising. Grant aid was the most significant, accounting for almost 50 per cent of income into the sector. Stations reported that the 50 per cent limit on funding from any one source had not been prohibitive and stations were receiving funding from a diversity of sources. Likewise, the six minute per hour restriction on advertising was not seen as proving prohibitive, in that no station was sourcing that amount of advertising anyway. In keeping with a general trend across Europe, community stations were moving away from this source of income. Members of the Community Radio Forum (CRF or "The Forum", see Chapters 3 and 4) recognised the important role the Community Radio Funding Scheme (later the Community Radio Support Scheme, CRSS) had played in the development of the sector. Arising from that meeting, however, the Forum identified two specific areas of development that it wished to see included in any BCI support scheme, namely, training and ethos promotion.

In this section, the focus is on the ethos of training and development that the community radio sector has demonstrated over the years. Stemming from this, a strong partnership was established with the BCI and this is outlined. Finally, programming itself is discussed, in particular the BCI initiative, New Adventures in Broadcasting, and the involvement of community radio stations in the scheme.

In terms of community radio in Ireland, sooner or later one always goes back to the AMARC Europe Charter (see appendix). Like all cornerstone documents, it provides a solid grounding of the key priorities for a sector. For community radio in general, the Charter established as an objective the provision of access to training and education for both community broadcasters and the community served at large. Point 2 of the AMARC Europe Charter states that community radio stations:

> provide access to training, production and distribution facilities; encourage local creative talent and foster local traditions; and provide programmes for the benefit, entertainment, education and development of their listeners. (See appendix).

This particular objective echoes that of the BCI in many ways. The Charter was indeed adopted by the then IRTC in 1994, at the beginning of the pilot project. The principle of development is reflected in the BCI Community Radio Policy and the fact that the Commission always seeks commitments in relation to the provision of training from aspirant community radio groups. It is inscribed in BCI policy on training and development that:

> The Commission attaches great importance and weight to the development of training and will pursue this on two levels. Firstly at a strategic level, the Commission will encourage and challenge the sector to develop sustainable enterprise-led training initiatives which exemplify good practice and which contribute to the overall development of industry standards and sectoral competencies. Secondly, the Commission will be open to supporting and responding to individual on the ground training initiatives emanating form the sector (BCI, 2000).

Put simply, this underlines the fact that the BCI strongly believes in supporting community radio broadcasters to achieve their objectives through a network and partnership approach. For the BCI looking to implement this policy, the Community Radio Forum was a natural partner, and the principles of supporting training and development found a real echo with the Community Radio Forum, now CRAOL (see Chapter 4).

So this is how it all began – CRAOL on the one hand and the BCI on the other looking to develop the sector and to support that development respectively. The first strategic support mechanism to be established was the Community Radio Support Scheme (CRSS). This has two key objectives, namely, station evaluation and development and networking, and these are described below.

As more community radio stations have been licensed since the end of the pilot project in 1997, the community radio sector in Ireland has been growing and maturing. The sector was becoming better established – volunteers were being sourced, programmes were being made and aired, and training was being delivered. The question which was surfacing for community radio activists, however, was "how well are we doing?" In order to provide the beginning of an answer beyond anecdotal evidence, the Commission and the Community Radio Forum agreed and devised a new support initiative called the Community Radio Support Scheme (CRSS). The main premise of the scheme was to enable networking opportunities, based on the premise that there is value in sharing respective initiatives and accomplishments. Because of the geographical spread of stations, and also because these are busy environments, there was a sense of isolation, of not knowing who, at the other end of the country, might be facing similar challenges, or who might be able to help in selected initiatives. Getting together to discuss these issues therefore was a positive move forward to break that isolation. The coordinating committee of the Community Radio Forum needed some support to organise these meetings which were operational as much as strategic (e.g. a crucial meeting on funding strategies held in Bow Street, Dublin in 2000). Some funding was therefore allocated to support networking events such as the Forum meetings, and the more operational committee meetings.

The other key initiative under the CRSS was the establishment of funding initiatives relating to the development and evaluation of individual stations. Under this strand, funding is made available to stations wishing to conduct either an internal or an external evaluation of their operations. The BCI sees evaluation as a very effective method of supporting the development of community stations. Internal evaluations tend to focus the organisational development of a station. Practical examples include facilitated workshops aiming to develop a mission statement, research funding policies, increase overall planning and evaluation, develop a volunteer policy, etc. External evaluations aim notably at developing the involvement of the community served, or gauging the profile of the listernership. Both the evaluation and the networking aspect of the CRSS highlighted a need to create a platform to share experiences and ideas. From there, the idea of organising a training event for all volunteers in community stations was formed.

In June 2001, Raidió Corca Baiscinn based in Kilkee, Co. Clare, organised the first ever Community Radio Training Féile. The Training Féile (see Chapter 4) was a weekend gathering during which representatives from community radio stations all over the country as well as aspirant groups converged on Kilkee to attend workshops in digital editing, volunteer policy, libel, programme production, webcasting, community management, funding strategies and many more. The Féile was also an opportunity to network and to share valuable experience. Over 80 staff and volunteers attended and the event was evaluated very positively. Minister for Communications Síle De Valera attended dinner on the final evening of the event. The event was a resounding success, and there was unanimous agreement that the event had not only provided an opportunity for training but also for networking between stations. The high level of participation and exposure was a departure for the sector and it was decided to turn this gathering into an annual event.

The following year, Connemara Community Radio hosted the Féile in Letterfrack, Co. Galway. The number of workshops on offer was increased and the number of attendees also increased to 120, an illustration of the needs of the sector in terms of training and networking. The model had been found for a successful and dynamic training event that could fit the needs of a majority of volunteers and community broadcasters. In 2003, the Féile was held in Cork Campus Radio, with significant names like John Quinn, RTÉ facilitating a workshop on documentary making, and Volunteering Ireland making a presentation on the contemporary volunteering landscape. In 2004, the Féile moved to Dublin, under the organisation of NEAR Fm. A record number of workshops were held (28), as well as a record number of participants. A debate was organised on the contribution that community radio can make to the voiceless, and the Chairperson of AMARC International delivered a keynote address at the opening of the three-day event. The year 2005 saw the Féile move to Limerick and it was preceded by an international academic conference on the theme "Community Radio: People, Places and Processes". Many of the speakers remained in the city to attend the Féile and they participated in the workshops and activities adding different valuable perspectives. (Their papers are available on www.rrc.mic.ul.ie.) In 2006 the Féile headed north to Inishowen, Co. Donegal and, once again, the scope of training and the breadth of experiences shared increased significantly. The Féile is therefore going from strength to strength and is a widely anticipated event in the sector, as it provides a unique opportunity for a large number of community broadcasters and volunteers to meet and exchange experiences, it's practical and useful, and is agreed by all participants to be a most enjoyable weekend.

Because of community radio's ethos and its specific mandate, training has always sat very comfortably in community radio. In the early days of the IRTC pilot project, community groups, broadcasters and activists had already identified the development of skills as an intrinsic part of community development, and that community radio would serve as a useful tool for that job. Other, more systematic and strategic approaches to training were to follow. Each of these aimed at meeting the needs of specific individuals and groups, for example community radio volunteers and community groups associated with the station while also servicing the requirements of the community radio sector itself, most significantly through the development of the Community Radio Forum which developed into CRAOL.

The refreshing perspective held by the community radio sector on the importance of training and development is the utter belief that training is simply the right thing to do. In many ways, it positions the sector as one of the more unusual ones, in that training is an objective value, rather than something which is only useful if it offers some immediate "return on investment". Stephanie Comey reports:

> As Training and Development Officer, I never had to convince them that training was a sound investment. Those involved in community radio always saw the benefits that good training brings and recognised the merit of investing not only financially but also in terms of time, a commodity often more rare than money in the community radio sector. I only had to find ways to enable them to provide appropriate training for their needs rather than convince them of the need for training.

Most of the priorities that the BCI had developed for the industry over time happened to also be community radio priorities, such as induction training, development and sustainability of skills for volunteers, management development, and last, but not least, accreditation of training. The relationship between the community radio movement in Ireland and its regulatory body, the BCI, has been positive and beneficial on both sides and could be usefully replicated in other jurisdictions. The early spirit of experimentation that was so strong during the pilot scheme of 1994–1997 has survived and leads to innovation and co-operation. The desire by all parties to see the community radio project succeed and spread throughout the country drives the close co-operation between the two bodies and this close relationship is remarked upon by outsiders, often to the extent of disbelief.

Accreditation has always been a key objective of the Commission, and the idea behind that is simply to ensure that people have transferable skills that they can use in a work context and develop. On the community radio side, accreditation of training had been flagged as a priority as early as the pilot project evaluation stage and this was highlighted in independent research carried out in stations involved in the pilot scheme (Dillon and Ó Siochrú, 1997). In 2002, the Forum became a registered centre for the Further Education Training Accreditation Council (FETAC), which meant that accredited training could now be accessed through stations (see Chapter 4). The Commission also worked with the Forum in the development of a new FETAC module in community radio. This module was written by community radio practitioners and serves as a useful and comprehensive introduction to the specificities of community broadcasting.

A lot of work has been undertaken by CRAOL on the accreditation front and the crowning achievement of accrediting people as trainers for the community radio sector itself was realised in early 2005. The course, certified by the Irish Institute of Training and Development (IITD) is a four-day long workshop which includes presentation skills, awareness of learning styles and other key elements enabling adequate training to others. Coupled with the large amount of work which went into writing and developing a curriculum for community radio broadcasters, this means that the sector owns a strategic, long-term policy on training and development. All of this is also an achievement of the CRSS and the faith that the BCI has shown in supporting the development of this sector. Over the years, since the end of the pilot project, there has been a steady accrual in the monies allocated to the sector.

In 1995, the Commission established a programming initiative aimed at encouraging the independent radio sector, both commercial and community, to select and showcase specially crafted, original productions for radio. The New Adventures in Broadcasting initiative (named such after an R.E.M. album) allocated funding for the development and production of new and innovative programming, of the type that might not otherwise be made. As funding is a key issue for community radio, the budgets allocated for programming have not traditionally been very large, with monies being used for other purposes such as training and outreach work. The New Adventures in Broadcasting initiative therefore became one of the only sources of funding available for developing professional programming abilities within a station.

The community radio sector in Ireland used the funding well, and was instrumental in the success of the scheme. Indeed, Connemara Community Radio won four awards in the competition over seven years. Other stations which accessed funding for new programmes include Wired Fm, Flirt Fm, Raidió na Life, Dublin South Fm, Raidió Corca Baiscinn, Inishowen Community Radio and NEAR Fm. In the final round of the scheme, in December 2004, newly licensed stations such as Dundalk Fm and WDAR were successful in securing funding.

The types of programmes funded were very varied indeed, with music tuition through Irish, documentaries on local craftsmen or artists, outreach initiatives with youth and students to name but a few. The quality was outstanding, and there is no doubt that the scheme encouraged and motivated volunteers and staff members to make innovative, creative and valuable programmes. The scheme provided the opportunity for hard-pressed volunteers and paid members of staff to realise some of their creative broadcasting potential by providing the funds and impetus to tackle long-term, time-consuming projects. The scheme became defunct with the arrival of a funding mechanism to promote public service programming within the independent broadcasting sector. The Sound and Vision Scheme, as it is called, provides a serious and welcome cash injection to community radio stations which can provide programmes of excellence in areas such as Irish culture, heritage, language and experience.

Over the years, community radio in Ireland has proven its strength and its vision. Its development has been intricately linked to the development of its staff and volunteers. By prioritising training and the development of individuals as a tool for the development of the community served, the community radio sector has indeed created and sustained a culture of learning. The benefits of evaluation and training for moving forward have long been accepted and promoted in the sector, making it flexible and adaptable to change – a must in a sector where there is a high turnover of volunteers, and where sourcing funding is a constant challenge.

PART THREE

Personal Reflections

12

CRY in the Afternoon:
The Early Days in Youghal

Noel Cronin
(in conversation with Rosemary Day)

I'm trying to roll back the years but I can only go back as far as 1971. I built a little transmitter here and we operated it out of my garage up at home. I suppose I was no more than 14 or 15 at the time. I was always interested in radio. My father was an electrician and, before I started in the ESB, I was working in a local radio and television shop here. We started it up as a lark every Sunday evening in my garage, just a fun kind of thing, playing music. That was myself and a few of my friends – Michael McCarthy, Ed Geary and Niall Callaghan – we started broadcasting out of the garage at home. We knew full well we were pirates and we were terrified operating it. We used to say to each other, "Look, the Minister for Posts and Telegraphs is going to walk in the door any minute and we're all heading for six months in Mountjoy, without a shadow of a doubt".

It was mostly as a summer thing that we started and we were noted for going on the air every day between two o'clock and four or five o'clock in the evening, whenever the notion would take us. It was all medium wave, on 310 medium wave back then. It was a great take around town because, what must be remembered is that at the time, there was no other station operating. Basically, from the radio perspective, we saw an opening because up until recently radio in this country was archaic. There was only RTÉ from Cork and RTÉ from Dublin and they gave a very limited service. The idea was starting to catch on in England with the independent radios starting to open up at around the same time. Listening here in Youghal you could receive a lot of them on the medium wave and the pirate scene was still going in Cork. Mostly what they were doing in Cork city was playing wall-to-wall or back-to-back music. The sort of stuff you got in night clubs, that sort of thing, and that was a great take because there was no local radio.

We were all involved in the Junior Chamber of Commerce at this time and we had plans to start a local community radio service. We wanted to try to go legally so we got on to the local TDs about getting a licence but nobody was interested at all. Nobody knew what we were on about at all, so the whole idea fell apart when we got a very negative response from authority.

It died a kind of a death here in Youghal until, amazingly enough, RTÉ themselves revived it in 1978. They had their RTÉ community wagon around the place. Now what that was, was a portable studio. They would rig up an aerial and a transmitter in a remote part of town and they situated the wagon with the studio in it in a central part of town, down by the town hall in fact. They would form a local committee and they would get local programmes, interviewing local personalities, that kind of thing. They would run the radio service for a week and then, after the week, they would pull out and go to some other town and form another committee and do the whole lot all over again. It was a marvellous take, naturally everybody listened in to it and, when RTÉ went, a few of us got together and said, "Look, this idea of community radio could work in a town like Youghal". If the truth be known, I think RTÉ was responsible for starting a lot of pirate stations around the country in that way.

A crowd of us got together and we had a meeting advertised by word of mouth. So there were four of us who took it on – Tony Hannon, Barty Murphy, Conor O'Reilly and myself. I had a lot of the gear as I was involved in the disco scene at the time. We had no premises so we asked around and we asked any fellow living up in the hills or anywhere at all for an old shed or an old shack or something like that. You see we needed an out-of-the-way location and we eventually happened on Paddy and Eileen Connolly's place. They were living up by the golf club in a farm house in Knockaverry. It was an old grain store and we got the attic in it. They were living in the house along side it but there were sheds adjoining it and they said, "Look, ye can have the attic there and whatever ye want to do, belt away!" Myself, I'm belting away since.

We started off just playing records but what we found very soon was that the real community came in then. People started looking to us for advice if they wanted to find out what was on around the place and we very soon found that we had a load of volunteers coming up to the station. We had people that wanted to get involved in the thing. We had local clubs and organisations who wanted coverage and so we found that we were on a couple of days a week and we found that we had to extend our hours. Originally we came on for just an hour a day but we had to increase that due to demand. We found that we had to extend our broadcasting to four or five hours a day to accommodate all this. Local clubs, organisations, everybody got involved. Right from the beginning it was called Community Radio Youghal, or CRY for short. We used have a jingle which went out with the sound of a baby crying and a voice over announcing "CRY! CRY! CRY! CRY in the Afternoon!" Our philosophy here was, and my philosophy still is, "Bringing the People Together". What community radio is all about, I firmly believe, is a community looking at itself, examining itself and portraying itself in a positive light.

The way we used run it was, the four of us used to sit down every week and plan out what we were going to do for the week.

One thing led to another, we got the local council involved. They were mad to get involved in it actually, even though the whole thing was illegal, but nobody spoke about the legalities of it. The council was not at all worried, we actually reported the council meetings and we did church services as well, right from the start. We started on the Fourth of July, American Independence Day, 1979.

We had a home-made kit, all we had basically were two record players and one tape recorder and one microphone, that was it, nothing else. We started to get into the live outside broadcasts and all that kind of thing, everything we had was homemade. The kit we made up was so heavy it took three of us to carry it but we managed. We rigged up loudspeakers around the town for the processions, just so everyone could hear.

We once had what we found to be a very successful programme, it was called *Pa and Nooch on Tour*. Pa and Nooch were two characters, Nooch was a fisherman, a very well-known gentleman here in town and Pa was Paddy Mulcahy, now deceased, unfortunately. They were both very well known characters around the town. One of them came up with this very simple idea that bringing some fellow up to the radio, a radio studio or doing an interview with them was very intimidating for somebody who had never spoken into a microphone. A lot of people were shy, so they hit upon the idea, why not go down into their local environment, go down into the local pub at night time, sit down with a microphone and sidle up to the fellow in the bar? He's with his friends, he's got a pint in front of him and he'll talk away to beat the band. That was the idea and the thing literally took off. What they did was, they went around and they started it off by interviewing the publican, they got the history of the pub. Then all the clientele would be coming in and they interviewed one or two of the locals coming in and the locals of course would always have a story. The psychology of it was that the local chap that was in there, he was among all his friends, he had a pint and everything was going well with a big fire crackling in the corner. He was at home and he just sat down and off he went, he literally poured his heart out for us. We did a lot of that kind of brilliant programming in the early days.

We had a lot of fun too. We had a fellow on the air, up in Eileen Connolly's attic in Knocknaverry, in the very early days and he used produce a tea-time programme of requests – dedications, local happenings, local news. He might bring up a local character and interview him, that kind of thing. It would go on great but he was a fierce witty guy altogether, his name was Aiden O'Doherty. It was kind of an open secret at the time where we were broadcasting from. Everybody knew where the studio was but nobody said it, because the police and the post office could be down top of us like a ton of bricks and close us down, although we were never raided actually. This particular guy came on air one day and he said, "Today ladies and gentlemen, today, we're coming from Capel Island". The following day he comes on and says, "Today", says he, "we're coming from the top of the clock", like that, as a laugh. But this person wrote in to say, "Dear Aiden, ye should have stayed out in Capel Island because when ye were out in Capel Island last week the reception was much better". Things like that were funny, people honestly believed what you told them over the air. You know they honestly believed it, which they wouldn't do today, as they are much more sophisticated now.

We found that our coverage was wider than we had thought. We found that more and more communities around East Cork and West Waterford were actually tuning in to us. They wanted us to come out and do the same thing for them, to book their local community hall and do a programme from there. So, we found that there was pressure on us to extend our range, to build better equipment, to do what we were doing, only bigger and better.

We went on from 1979 until the government brought in the existing legislation in 1988. The government brought in a ruling that all pirate radio stations should come off the air if they were interested in getting a licence, so we obeyed. In the interim, we had developed ourselves to become a community service. We were after moving down from Connolly's to a premises in town, right alongside the Gate, in Frank Irwin's. We had purchased VHF equipment and various bits of outside broadcasting equipment as well, which made the job easier for ourselves. We were excited and ready to go back on air, but we were five years, five years waiting and lobbying and waiting to go back on air.

13

Community Radio Memories:
Dublin South Fm

Mike Purcell

Dublin South FM was the first licensed community station to go on air in Dublin in June 1995. A few things happened before that, however ...

In the Beginning

"I see here there's a group talking about setting up a local radio station in Dundrum. You're always messing about at tape recorders – maybe you should go along and see what it's all about ...", my wife said, talking over a raised newspaper in 1986 and that was how it all started for me. I went to the meeting convened by local residents associations and Jack Byrne fired everybody with his enthusiasm for local involvement and empowerment. A committee was set up and off we went hurtling into a future which was to be full of excitement, meetings, bureaucracy, rage, political lobbying, euphoria, disappointment, meetings, a five-year "hold-off" by the IRTC, more meetings, false alarms, plans, community involvement, shares, fundraising, building, wiring, support, training, *the licence*, until, finally ... we were "on the air" from Dundrum.

My mind is awash with memories of the sheer thrill of it all.

First Steps

"But how did you start off?" I hear you cry. Well, the committee started with weekly meetings in the local Ballinteer Community School. A tidal wave of ideas swept over each meeting – *everybody* had an idea about what we should be doing. These were finally broken down into tasks, and people went off into the night, clutching their notes and bubbling with enthusiasm. As word spread, more volunteers began to come on board. But we needed to get to grips with the mechanics of radio, and train a corps of actual broadcasters.

I was happy to dive into this area. My own interest is in sound, technical stuff and "programming", having been honed by years in the Irish Tape Recording Society. A subsequent ten-year stint of studio building plus "doing the desk" for a monthly tape magazine for the blind provided further useful experience. The tape magazine *Scéal Beo*, which means the living story, is, I believe, still going strong. Anyway, a programme group was formed and we started by interviewing each other – sitting in schoolroom desks – on a Marantz recorder which had been gathering dust at home. Soon we were brave enough to interview total strangers, and we began to gather the results.

Enter Gerry Roe, a distinguished ex-pirate. A good book, *Radio, Radio*, by Peter Mulryan (1988) tells the story of independent, local, community and pirate radio in Ireland. You will get a good flavour of the times and we are in there, listed as Dundrum Community Radio, which, of course, we were, back in the good old pirate days. Gerry had a small triangular studio – triangular because it was the actual corner of his living room – and there we began editing, linking our interviews together into programmes on tape. Next, these tapes needed to be transmitted.

Transmitter Thingys

We heard on the grapevine that a transmitter and aerial might be for sale, and thus came into possession of a mysterious box, plus a gold coloured thing, looking like part of a broken bedstead. This, we were informed, was a Sherman dipole – a high-class aerial.

Local historian and author Jim Nolan joined our crew and he had three very useful things for local radio: (1) a wide knowledge of local history, with a book already published, *The Changing Face of Dundrum*, an ideal source of local history programmes; (2) a huge collection of music, on tape and disc; and (3) a motorised television aerial which could be rotated from a control box beside his hi-fi. I had reckoned, in my innocence, that "an aerial was an aerial", i.e. it could be used to transmit as well as to receive. If we plugged our transmitter into his TV aerial surely it could *transmit* our signal. We could also point it towards Rathfarnham, about two miles away, to see if we could reach their community. I remember being on my hands and knees on his dining room carpet, secretly hoping that the transmitter would not explode, or burn out his TV aerial. There was no "Plan B".

At last, a phone call from Rathfarnham: our tape could be heard in the New World, but not too well. There was a hill between us and Rathfarnham – we needed a booster station – send for Marconi!

We had another tiny, ex-taxi transmitter we thought could maybe help. One of our founding leading lights, Tony Duggan, lived right on the brow of the offending hill, on Barton Road East, and he happily accepted the Sherman dipole onto his roof, and donated his garage to the cause. A small portable FM radio was tuned to receive the signal from Jim Nolan's TV aerial, and its headphone output fed the tiny taxi transmitter. My home hi-fi tuner was brought into the garage and the digits set to our new required frequency. The taxi transmitter was then adjusted until the programme coming from Main Street, Dundrum was heard on the tuner. Bingo, we were in business! Thus for a short period we ran on two frequencies, 94.8 Fm for the natives of Dundrum, and relayed on 96.7 Fm to the outlying tribes on the hills of Rathfarnham. Our paper-and-string communications network was up and running.

Our next task was to "automate" the operation. Two C-90 programme tapes were loaded into an AIWA twin-deck cassette player, set to "repeat". This unit came on at 8.00 pm and went off at midnight, using a time switch. We could now demonstrate our wares to the community. Notices appeared around the area advising the locals that the New Dawn had arrived. Radio had been reclaimed: it was not just for *them*, it was for *us* as well!

Premises, Premises (1)

We talked to SUCCES, the local job creation group, and convinced them that our aims and objectives to help the local community coincided precisely with theirs. They agreed to give us a small room off Main Street, at the back of a premises they were using. A rickety dipole was mounted on the roof (parked in a tin bucket with strategically-placed concrete blocks) and Jim Nolan finally got to use his TV aerial again.

A "studio" was assembled in the room, the centre-piece being a Maplin mixer, purchased in London on a day trip. The room also contained the transmitter on a high shelf (not a good idea at all!) and we learned the hard way that radio frequencies leak into every crevice of cheap audio gear. Mysterious "hums" could be cured only by routing cables on strange and wondrous paths. Zero-hum positions were discovered, and the cable nailed exactly where it lay. A rough schedule was devised, and soon a stream of volunteers began to tickle the tail of the radio dinosaur.

To OB or not to OB?

Somebody had borrowed a radio mike, and with great excitement we sent two young volunteers out on to Main Street, Dundrum – about 50 feet around the corner from our studio – to conduct our very first Outside Broadcast (OB). Clutching a ghetto blaster, for programme cues, they accosted a lady who, quite reasonably, refused to believe that these teenagers were actually live on air. Her face, when she heard the ghetto blaster introduce the team, and then her own voice coming from it, was a sight to be seen. Baffled by technology and possibly by the audacity of 1980s teenagers, she departed unsteadily down the street and may even still be scratching her head. For me it brought home the immediacy and intimacy of local, community radio.

We started looking around for community activities to get involved in. The annual Dundrum Festival needed a PA system and we offered to arrange and run this from a caravan. Needless to say, we managed to insert live interviews and music shows in between Glamorous Granny and Bonny Baby competitions – just to show that "the radio group" was alive and well. During one ferocious downpour, the year *before* a caravan had become available, we were forced to set up our DJ/PA equipment *under* the stage – the only dry spot for miles around. Another year saw us squeeze the PA gear into the back of a car from which we operated quite successfully.

We recorded events and bands, from the Dublin Symphony Orchestra in stereo to a local history walkabout, from excavations as they were in progress at Dundrum Castle to the Tour de France as it passed through the capital and lots, lots more. These were all edited back at "the station" and duly appeared in our taped "Community Report" programme. Things were really beginning to move, or so we thought.

Pirates

At this time, Dublin was saturated with pirate radio stations, many coming on-air at weekends when their owners were off school. Bands of pirate brigands roamed the capital, stealing anything that could assist transmission. Stories abounded of transmitters locked in underground bunkers, and Radio Dublin's mountain aerial was alleged to be painted green, and concealed up a tree to ensure its survival.

Knowing, however, that legitimacy would be a future requirement for our station, we made sure to advise all the local politicians of our bona fides, promising to go off air when the long awaited legislation was enacted, and indicating that a "proper licence" was our ultimate aim.

Premises, Premises (2)

The local parish priest, Rev. Joe Fagan, was approached and, having heard our plans, generously offered us an unused room in the local school. With our profile increasing, we started gathering community shareholders and supporters. With the money raised we designed and built our first "real" studio in Holy Cross School, with separate work areas for production, broadcasting and administration and with much-needed sound proofing. Little did we know that this was the first of *three* studios we would eventually have to build as we were constantly on the move.

No Joy

Suddenly, like a death in the family, came the sickening crunch. Despite a string of promised launch dates, the IRTC decided to put community radio "on hold" *sine die,* and then the hard, hard slog as we fought to keep the dream alive. Biweekly meetings were to continue for a full incredible five years but without a launch date we could hardly look a shareholder in the eye. Not a licence in sight, and community enthusiasm slowly drained into the gutters. Controlled rage at bureaucracy turned out to be the power behind our survival. We were a community of real people with a real need and we could not be turned off like a tap. We just would not go away.

Our six-week training course, complete with our own illustrated hand-out sheets, was now in operation, turning shy "I'll never be able to do this" novices into enthusiastic radio operators. People of all ages, from teenage boys to grey-haired old ladies, donned headphones, scanned their scripts with one eye, and the level meters with the other, as they questioned their friends intently about their activities. "But when do we go on air?" was always their question, for which we had no answer for oh, so long.

Roadshows

In the doldrums, we searched for novel ways to generate community involvement and to keep our own spirits up. In exchange for printing and distributing what seemed to be 900 million leaflets, we obtained the loan of a caravan from a local hire company and set up a roadshow in the six surrounding shopping centres – one every Saturday for six weeks.

PA speakers on top of the caravan relayed interviews and live music from local guests as we "tried out" local radio on the shoppers. Their reaction was inspiring, with many shoppers complaining that they couldn't pick us up on their car radios. Our leaflets explained why, and asked for support.

A Schools Art Competition was next. Children from several local schools were asked to send in a drawing to illustrate "My Very Own Radio Station". Hundreds of entries flooded in and the winners were given their prizes and "interviewed" on tape for a simulated Broadcast Weekend. Our volunteers were gaining invaluable experience.

Interviews and music were all very well in small spurts but could we do it non-stop for hours at a time, like "real radio"? We

determined to find out. A Simulated Radio Weekend was announced, and a full schedule of programmes and presenters was
set up. An Exhibition was also mounted, and members of the public and all politicians were invited along for "tea with radio".

"Live" programmes commenced at 9.00 am in our recently
completed studios in Holy Cross School, and continued until 9.00
pm. Roundtable discussion programmes were held, wrapped up,
and hand-overs made to music programme presenters in the studio next door. Heaving bodies moved about clutching their
marked-up schedules and scripts. No room in our cramped studio
meant we had to relay pictures from our camera to a TV set next
door and programmes were heard on loudspeakers. Reports
from the politicians and tea-drinking well-wishers were that it
sounded rather convincing.

After day one, Saturday, we knew we could do it for real. Day
two was the icing on the cake, we could make and *eat* radio now!

All at Sea

Then someone had a brainwave: "Let's all go to sea!" We decided
that our annual "state of the union" meeting would be held on
board the Stena ferry bound for Holyhead, Wales. This would be
a shot in the arm for our volunteers who were beginning to feel
that community radio would *never* come. There's something
about a meeting on the high seas that inspires camaraderie and
enthusiasm. Everything went swimmingly (groan), including a slide
show and a suitably-edited video of that Simulated Broadcast
Weekend. A few hours in Holyhead, and back home again that
evening: we were ready to launch community radio with pure
adrenalin-power, if that were possible.

My memories of this next period blur into a melange of meetings, events and ever more meetings. Jack Byrne, of what was to
become NEAR Fm, was a tower of strength, enthusiasm and organisation. I remember a meeting of Dublin postulants in the Man-

sion House where we all carved up the map of Dublin and agreed our respective areas for presentation as a solution to the Commission of the IRTC. The Lord Mayor of the day, Mr. Seán Haughey, kindly spoke, provided refreshments and agreed to become patron of the Dublin City Radio Group.

Next, Jack arranged a seminar at Dublin City University (DCU) at which the Minister for Communications, Mr. Ray Burke, gave the keynote address. He said all the right things, and seemed to have a grasp of what we were about. "Community groups should set about applying for licences," he said. Things seemed to be coming together at last. But, of course, they were not. The Minister's ideas and those of the newly-formed IRTC did not coincide. This applying for licences was *his* idea, not *theirs* ...

Then Jack introduced us to AMARC, the World Association for Community Radio Broadcasters, and we took on board their excellent 10-point Charter (see appendix), which reflected all our aspirations for community empowerment. We were pleased to see that community radio had an international dimension, and that our concerns were so alike. There was great pride in the fact that Dublin was hosting the bi-annual AMARC convention in University College Dublin (UCD), actually within our catchment area. Delegates came from more countries than we knew existed. "Where, in God's name, is Burkino Faso?" I wondered, having just chatted to two delegates clad in brightly coloured robes. I headed quickly, but discreetly, for the nearest atlas.

It gradually became apparent that democracy, unlike the comfortable environs of Western Europe, existed in only a minority of these countries. The search for freedom and justice involving the use of community radio had a decided, but quite understandable, revolutionary whiff about it. Seeing the conservative chairman of the IRTC, Mr Justice Henchey, at one of these sessions, I wondered at his reaction. In hindsight, it's possible that his exposure to what may have superficially appeared as a bunch of lefty revolutionaries may well have put the tin hat on the chances of

Irish community radio licences being issued on his watch. Whatever about that, the reasons advanced by the IRTC for not issuing
community radio licences at the time were truly inexplicable.

Meetings with politicians continued unabated, but unfortunately
without result. There was a brief flurry as an all-Dublin licence was
announced. Not *local* community radio, we thought, but maybe a
start. A group was formed, a meeting was held in the Shelbourne
Hotel, and a reasonable application was made, but it turned out to
be unsuccessful in the face of an alternative group. Dark mutterings
about people being on the inside track ensued. An article in the
satirical magazine *Phoenix* appeared to confirm our suspicions.

Three Dublin groups then approached Denis O'Brien of 98FM,
following the publication of an article by him which looked sympa-
thetically on the concept of local radio. A proposal to use existing
waiting community radio frequencies as opt-outs, with 98FM as the
main umbrella sustaining service, appeared to have some merit.
"We might not have to apply for a licence," went the thinking. But
like all community radio projects around that time, it gradually fizzled out.

Nirvana, or similar

The patron saint of community radio in Ireland turned out to be
Michael D. Higgins. With a change of Government, this newly-
appointed Minister of Communications opened his files, came
upon Community Radio, and saw that it was good! With one
wave of his magic wand, he unveiled a new Broadcasting Bill, un-
did the five year log-jam, and instructed the IRTC, under its new
chief executive, to begin the licensing procedure.

Expressions of interest – and, by God, were we interested –
were invited yet again by the IRTC and ours rocketed into their
offices. The IRTC had a new boss. Mr. Niall Stokes, the founder
and editor of *Hot Press*, Ireland's rock music magazine, was appointed the chairperson of the commission of the IRTC. It

seemed that the known world had rotated several degrees left on its axis, and we were mighty pleased with the result.

I remember consuming the excellent IRTC *Guide to Licence Applications* and being quite impressed as the application guided your thoughts towards all the facets that needed to be addressed in developing a radio station from a basket of ideas and enthusiasms. We prepared our brief, practised our delivery, manufactured our powerpoint slides, produced our logo, crossed our fingers and made for the oral hearings, feeling not a little like clients of the Nuremberg Trials. The hearings layout helped to reinforce this idea, as we sat in a line, angled towards a central screen, with the IRTC committee facing us on the opposite side. Our presenter played a blinder, and various supplementary questions were then addressed to the experts – us! After it was all over, we got some unofficial comments that we hadn't done too badly but proper breathing did not return until the letter arrived, advising that we could get ready to sign a contract to broadcast. We had attempted Beecher's Brook and had succeeded!

Premises, Premises (3)

Quick flashback: Used as we were to unpleasant surprises, we received another unexpected setback. We had recently been informed that the school in which our new studios had been built with such enthusiasm and through the substantial financial outlay of shareholders funds, would not allow us to broadcast from there. With a licence in the offing this seemed remarkably like a terminal event. No premises meant no licence.

Our station manager, by now skilled in negotiating minefields, managed to convince the owner of an old building known as the PYE Centre that a community radio station on his premises would enhance his standing in the locality. Against all odds, Mr Aidan Stanley – who had previously dabbled with local radio – allowed us the use of five rooms, rent-free, and earned our undying gratitude. We set to, and began to build our *second* studio and office complex. In a short number of weeks the interior was gutted, rebuilt, wired, tested and ready to go with three studios, two on-air and one for editing. All done by the same trio who had cut their teeth on the school studios only a short time before.

And so on Saturday, 5 June 1995, the sun shone extra brightly on the Dublin South Community Radio offices, located in the historic PYE Centre where, appropriately, radios had been produced in the nearby factory since the late 1930s, and all through the Emergency.

I had survived a Brian Farrell interview on national radio that morning, and had managed to get our station jingle played to the nation as the first Dublin community radio station. Local people had gathered in their finery to have a snack and hear the opening speeches from politicians, IRTC officials and our late chairman Tom Murchan. Our station was on-air from 2.00 pm and our first news bulletins carried snatches of the opening speeches – hurriedly extracted from the recording Marantz.

That tired old phrase "a new era had begun" seemed strangely appropriate.

The Business of Radio

Based on a Community Employment (CE or FÁS) scheme, we began to see the station evolve from a relatively amateur start-up to what was to become a more professional and businesslike operation. Suddenly "administration", an almost unknown activity, began to assume its own importance and the newly born "community radio animal" had to be fed and watered.

A plethora of new concerns hove arose as the FÁS staff were allocated to various necessary duties. Telephone bills, stationery, bank accounts, the Registrar of Friendly Societies, the auditor, copyright fees, insurance, the IRTC evaluation visits, board meetings, employment problems – was there really time to do radio as well as all that lot? Strangely, there was.

However, in our innocence, we had anticipated that a tidal wave of community groups would beat a path to our door, foaming with enthusiasm and demanding access to a microphone. Our job would be to take tea, reclining on an adjacent chaise longue, and direct them to the nearest studio, from which would pour forth radio of supreme excellence. It wasn't quite like that. Very few actually came. We realised that our job was to go out and *sell* the advantages of community radio to a public who had no feel for how it could be used. The Americans, on the other hand, *understood* local radio. Since the 1930s every small town had its own local station, and the colleges had their own stations as well. Small-scale local radio was normal in America; people in Ireland needed to be shown what it could do for them.

Successive Irish governments had kept a stranglehold on radio, to such a degree that people didn't know what to do with it when it arrived. Radio was passive. It was for *listening to*. Our next task was to go out and meet the community, to convince them that this new-fangled radio thing really had something to offer them to do. So, for the next year, we met every possible shade of community group. Some immediately grasped the potential and came on board enthusiastically. Others, well, some people just never seem to understand.

Programmes

Programmes started up OK, but gradually evolved from what *we* thought was necessary, to what *others* thought was necessary. We opened a Sunday "God Slot" to all the organised churches who produced an excellent cross-section of programmes. Personally, I'm still waiting to see radio creatively used to address those for whom organised religion has *no* meaning – i.e. those who aren't comfortably among the "saved".

The sight of three five-year-olds, clustered around a mike, reading their own poems and wearing enormous *Beyer* head-phones will always stay with me as the epitome of totally un-commercial radio. We organise and host a Schools Quiz, asking 10,000 questions, and every season we record and produce nine programmes locally and this has proven to be a major interactive success. A local traditional music programme, recorded in a nearby pub, produced about 65 programmes, gave each group a free demo-tape, and got an IRTC award for innovation.

Premises, Premises (4)

Our tenancy of the old PYE Centre was always going to be tem-porary – we had seen the plans for a shopping centre and hotel which were to be built there – but nobody was sure quite when we would have to vacate. Relatively suddenly, the site was sold to a large developer – who would eventually build the new Dundrum Town Centre – and we had three months to find a new home.

We approached the local authority of Dún Laoghaire Rath-down County Council who kindly allocated us two rooms in the Old School on Loreto Avenue. This was already a base for several other FÁS schemes and provided us not only with a good, sound premises, but one in which we were firmly rooted in and linked to our community. We now began, for the *third* time, the job of building a radio station from scratch.

Money was ultra tight, so we approached a small local builder to put a door between the two rooms, and divide up the second old classroom into three studios, a desk space and a small room to house the transmitter and logger. He put up studded partition, plastered on one side, and left all the rest to us. We filled the par-tition space with rockwool, cut with a garden shears, and covered it with fireproof tweed material stapled into position. This was a somewhat precarious job allowing for the nine-foot schoolroom ceilings but by now we had perfected the art of living on fresh air.

Chairs, filing cabinets and some carpet came from a Bank of Ireland office which was being renovated, and screened cable was left over from some factory wiring. A bag of XLR connectors came from a begging letter to Windmill Lane Studios who were, thankfully, upgrading to the moulded variety. The distinctly second-hand, main carpet was supplied by somebody's mother who was glad to get rid of it. A few spare lengths of the tweed covering were hung in one studio to absorb the sound.

Using advanced geometrical physics, we managed to cut up some circular Bank of Ireland workstations into two rectangular desks to take the sound mixers. The downside is that after a day pushing the electric jigsaw your drinking arm stiffens up and a week of enforced teetotal abstinence occurs. No pain, no gain. Finally the studios were built and painted, the new aerial was erected and, about a mile from our previous location, we were in business again. We had managed to stay on-air throughout the entire operation.

About four years on, we began to hear stories about the new Dundrum Town Centre – the biggest in Europe – to be built in the centre of Dundrum. The developers were anxious to assist some community groups by providing space in the new centre. We quickly made contact, supplied proposed layout drawings, and after about two years we got confirmation that we would be allocated a location on the fifth floor of this prestigious development. Ironically, our first real studios are buried somewhere below the new underground carpark. We set to, yet again, designing our layout and wiring details. We were able to provide for ethnic broadcasting for the growing immigrant population in the capital city. Our plans allow for either studio to go on-air independently so we can increase the hours and the reach we have to our growing and rapidly changing population. This is the *fourth* radio station we have built on almost no funds.

People

We have always been lucky to have a number of people with a range of disabilities involved in the station. Many arrived at our doors with no skills, a poor self-image, and low employment potential. They left with new personal dignity, new skills and greatly-improved job prospects. Several have since joined mainstream, commercial radio stations and other employment and we see this as a major success for the station. Community radio helps those who make programmes just as much as those who enjoy listening to them.

Transition Year students join in programmes and get invaluable work experience. Media students get their class projects on air. Kids get to broadcast to their mammies and neighbours. Retired people discuss their concerns and play their own kind of music which can no longer be found on the commercial airwaves. Young trainee journalists cover local news stories and then read them on air. Songwriters and emerging bands get their first breaks here in Dublin South – our *On the Verge* programme is a mecca for new Dublin talent. Ethnic groups broadcast in their own languages and get to communicate with their peers scattered throughout the area. Writers and poets display their wares and a *DJ for a Day* spot allows anyone to come on and play an hour of their choice of music. They arrive, fizzing with excitement and many stay, bitten by the community radio bug, to work on programmes which help to build the fabric and spirit of community in South County Dublin.

Real people are doing things that are important to themselves. This is real personal development in action. The community listens to its life being lived, and life gets a bit better for everyone. Like the Hokey Kokey, that's what it's all about!

14

Raidió na Life: Raidió na Réabhlóide

Fachtna Ó Drisceoil

In this chapter Fachtna Ó Drisceoil describes how Raidió na Life, Dublin's radio station for the community of Irish speakers in the capital city, got started, what it has meant to him personally and what the station is doing at the moment in terms of its aims and its programming. Recounting some of the highlights and on-air near misses that are part and parcel of community radio life, he pays tribute to the innovation and energy of some of the many hundreds of voluntary broadcasters who provide a modern radio service to Irish speakers in the capital. Predating TG4, Raidió na Life became a fertile training ground for many who went on to take up broadcasting professionally in TG4, RTÉ and elsewhere through English and through Irish.

> The word is out − if you want to hear the best of underground music of the Nineties, you tune into Maria Nic Oilebhaird ... even though she broadcasts entirely in the Irish language ... For her Tuesday night show is about the only slot on the official airwaves that you're likely to hear the hottest rap, grunge, techno, ragga, hardcore, trash and industrial music ... (*Sunday World,* 27 February 1994)

There's a cultural retaliation going on out there, on a grand scale, and Raidió na Life should be its loud-hailer. *(The Irish Times,* 15 March 1994*)*

Ba gheall le réabhlóid bheag tús chraoladh Raidió na Life i 1993. Tá sé deacair é a chreidiúnt anois ach b'é seo an chéad uair go raibh raon iomlán ceol comhaimseartha agus ceol le liricí Béarla á chraoladh, le cur i láthair i nGaeilge. B'é seo an chéad uair go raibh ceoilíní (focal a chum an chéad bainisteoir do "jingles") á gcraoladh ar stáisiún raidió Gaeilge, nó "promos" do chláracha, nó ceol aitheantais don Nuacht. Chuir teacht Raidió na Life go mór leis an díospóireacht faoi pholasaí craoltóireachta Raidió na Gaeltachta. Sna blianta tar éis do Raidió na Life teacht ar an aer thosaigh Raidió na Gaeltachta ag craoladh ceoilíní agus promos, ceol aitheantais don nuacht agus clár ceart ceoil chomhaimseartha. Agus i 2005 chuir RTÉ Raidió na Gaeltachta tús le hAnocht FM, seirbhís ceoil istoíche ar a gceadaítear amhráin le liricí Béarla. Tá méadú tagtha freisin ar líon na gclár a chraoltar as Baile Átha Cliath ar RTÉ Raidió na Gaeltachta. Nílim ag maíomh gurbh é Raidió na Life an t-aon chúis gur tharla na forbairtí seo, ach gach uile uair le blianta anuas go raibh díospóireacht faoi pholasaí ceoil Raidió na Gaeltachta, luaigh duine éigin sampla Raidió na Life.

Fiú lasmuigh de shaol na Gaeilge bhí tionchar nach beag ag Raidió na Life. Cuimhnigh ag an am sin nach raibh aon cheann de na stáisiúin pobail eile sa leabhar seo ar an aer. Bhí an dá stáisiún tráchtála i mBaile Átha Cliath ag spealladh amach popcheol lár-an-bhóthair 24 uair an cloig in aghaidh an lae. Bhí tuiscint ar leith ag an gcéad bhainisteoir, Rónán Ó Dubhthaigh, ar an mbearna a d'fhág sé seo do Raidió na Life. Diosc-mharcach gairmiúl agus iarchraoltóir leis an stáisiún bradach BLB (Bray Local Broadcasting) ba ea Rónán. Chreid sé go láidir sa pholasaí "Ceolta na Cruinne" mar a tugadh air – sainchlár ag díriú ar chinéal éagsúil ceoil chuile oíche den tseachtain. Bhí daoine áirithe ar an mBord Bainistíochta nár aithin roinnt de na cinéalacha ceoil seo mar cheol in aon chor, ach bhíodar leathan-aigeanta go leor cead a gcinn a thabhairt do na craoltóirí óga!

Bhíos féin ar dhuine de na craoltóirí óga sin ach ba bheag mo spéis sa cheol ailtéarnach – theastaigh uaim a bheith mar an chéad Brian Farrell eile. Nuair a chuaigh Raidió na Life ar an aer le ceadúnas sealadach le linn an Oireachtais i 1990, scaoileadh liom cúpla feasachán nuachta a léamh. Nuair a tháinig an stáisiún ar an aer i gceart i 1993 thosaíos ag cur eagrán amháin den irischlár *An Tuar Ceatha* i láthair chuile seachtain. Bhí Cáit Nic Aongusa mar chomhláithreoir liom ar feadh tamaill, agus mo chomleacaí ollscoile Treasa Harkin mar léiritheoir. An lá a bhfuair an t-aisteoir clúiteach Cyril Cusack bás bheartaíos gur chóir dúinn mír a dhéanamh faoi. Chuireas féin glaoch ar Mick Lally agus thoilig sé labhairt liom ar aer. Nuair a thosaigh an clár, chuireas mo ghuth ba shollúnta orm féin chun bás Cusack a fhógairt. Ansin thosnaíos ag cur Lally i láthair: "Agus ar an líne gutháin anois linn chun caint faoi Cyril Cusack tá... tá... an t-aisteoir...." Ar an nóiméad sin ní fhéadfainn cuimhneamh ar ainm ar bith ach Miley! Ní dheachaigh mé riamh isteach sa stiuideó ina dhiaidh sin gan gach ainm a bheith scríte síos agam, fiú dá mba le mo dhearatháir féin a bhíos chun caint leis!

Bhíos féin díreach i ndiaidh mo chéim ollscoile a chríochnú agus bhíos dí-fhostaithe. Roinnt seachtainí tar éis do Raidió na Life dul ar an aer fuaireas áit ar scéim FÁS an stáisiúin. Bhíos anois ag obair don stáisiún go hoifigiúl ar feadh 20 uair an chloig chuile sheachtain, cé go ndearna mé i bhfad níos mó ná sin i ndáiríre. Bhí riail ann nach raibh cead ag lucht na scéime cláracha a chur i láthair le linn a n-uaireanta oibre. Níor oibríos chomh crua, níor bhaineas oiread taitnimh, agus níor íocadh a laghad tuarastail liom i bpost ar bith ó shin! Bhaineas an-taitneamh as a bheith ábalta triail a bhaint as gach cineál oibre sa stáisiún: láithreoireacht cláracha cainte agus ceoil; léiriú cláracha agus fógraí tráchtála; meascadh fuaime; léitheoireacht nuachta agus mar sin de.

B'iontach an spiorad agus an fuinneamh a bhí sna craoltóirí. Bhuaigh Seosamh Ó Murchú duais Oireachtais don chlár cúrsaí reatha *Allagar na Cathrach* i 1995. I 1996 bhuaigh Marie Ní Chonchubhair duais Oireachtais don sraith *Mná ag an gCrosbhóthar*. Níor chualthas riamh cheana mná ag caint chomh hoscailte agus chomh hionraic ar chlár Gaeilge faoi chúrsaí pearsanta ar nós ailse brollaigh, colscaradh agus leispiachas. I mí na Samhna 1993 bhuaigh an stáisiún gradam sa chomórtas *Better Ireland Awards* de chuid Bhanc Aontas Éireann.

Ar nós gach uile stáisiún eile sa leabhar seo, bhíomar teoranta de shíor ag easpa acmhainní. Ach b'iontach an t-uaillmhian, an t-samhlaíocht agus an díograis a léirigh go leor craoltóirí. Cuimhním mar shampla ar an sraith-dhráma grinn *Slic Sleamhan agus Cás na bhFrídíní Marfacha* a scríobh agus a léirigh George Sharpson. Nó an craoladh beo a rinneamar ón mBád Farantóireachta idir Dún Laoghaire agus Holyhead, a bhuíochas dár sár-theicneoir Rónán Ó Fearaíl. Nó an seó bóthair *Seó Joe* a chuir Joe Reddington i láthair, ar bhonn deonach, cúig lá in aghaidh na seachtaine idir a 5.00i.n. agus 6.00i.n. Bhíodh *Agallamh na Seachtaine* le hÉamonn Ó Dónaill thar a bheith spéisiúl i gcónaí. Bhínn ag déanamh an deasc fuaime go minic do chlár dárbh ainm *Scoraíocht an Domhnaigh*, clár beo de cheol agus de sheanchas. An oíche áirithe seo bhí duine éigin tar éis a eagrú go mbeadh láithreoir nua ag teacht isteach ar an gclár, fear dárbh ainm Ó Súilleabháin. Ní raibh léiritheoir ar bith i láthair, ní raibh mo dhuine tar éis a bheith i stiuideó raidió riamh cheana agus bhí sé ar tí dul i mbun ceann de na cláracha is deacra le cur i láthair. Bhíos cinnte go mbeadh an rud ina thubaist. Ach ón nóiméad gur oscail sé a bhéal, bhí sé soiléir go raibh craoltóir nádúrtha, deisbhéalach tagtha chugainn isteach. "Tarraing isteach ansin níos giorra don tine" a déarfadh sé lena haoínna, agus táimse ag rá leat go gcreidfeá gur istigh i gcistin tí a bhí sé agus tú ag éisteacht leis.

Bhí an t-ádh linn comhairle den scoth a bheith ar fáil againn ó leithéidí Bhrian Mac Aongusa, iar-chraoltóir le RTÉ agus iar-stiúrthóir na gClár in RTÉ. Lá dá raibh an bainisteoir as láthair bhíos féin i gceannas an tí agus tháinig Brian isteach chun súil a choinneáil ar an áit. Thugamar faoi deara roinnt nóiméid roimh am nuachta nach raibh aon léitheoir nuacht tagtha. Bhí socrú againn le seomra nuachta 98FM ag an am go gcuirfeadh siad script Béarla ar fáil dúinn agus bhíodh ar an léitheoir nuachta é a aistriú roimh ré. Dúirt Brian go ndéanfadh sé an cúram, cé nach raibh fágtha ach cúpla nóiméad. Go luath ina dhiaidh sin chuala mé ag léamh na nuachta é, agus níor thugas aon rud ait faoi deara ach amháin go raibh sé ábhairín beag mall ina chuid cur i láthair. Is ina dhiaidh sin a fuair mé amach go raibh sé tar éis aistriú beo ar an aer a dhéanamh ar an script Béarla, go Gaeilge fhoirfe, nádúrtha.

Níl aon amhras orm ach gur chabhraigh mo thaithí i Raidió na Life liom dul chun cinn a dhéanamh i ngairm na craoltóireachta. Go deimhin, is liosta le háireamh na hiar-chraoltóirí de chuid Raidió na Life atá anois ag obair do RTÉ agus do chraoltóirí eile. An mó duine a bhfuil a fhios acu gur thosaigh an léitheoir nuachta Sharon Ní Bheoláin a gairm craoltóireachta ag cur *Seó Beo na nDéagóirí* i láthair ar Raidió na Life? I measc na n-iarchraoltóirí eile tá Aedin Gormley atá anois ina láithreoir ar RTÉ Lyric FM, tá Róisín Saxe ina láithreoir ar an stáisiún teilifíse popcheoil VH1, tá Sinéad Crowley ina tuairisceoir le Nuacht RTÉ agus tá Ruairí Mac an Iomaire ina thuairisceoir le Nuacht TG4, gan ach cúpla sampla a lua.

Tar éis dom bliain a chaitheamh ar an scéim FÁS, d'fhágas Raidió na Life chun céim mháistreachta a bhaint amach san ollscoil i nGaillimh. Ina dhiaidh sin d'oibrigh mé mar thuairisceoir nuachta ar TG4, mar thuairisceoir ar chláracha éagsúla do RTÉ, agus mar léiritheoir raidió do RTÉ. Thugas cúnamh ó am go ham do Raidió na Life, ach tuairim is sé bhlian ó shin thosnaíos ag éirí gníomhach sa stáisiún arís, agus táim ar an mBord Bainistíochta anois. Mar dhuine a bhain an-tairbhe as Raidió na Life nuair a bhíos níos óige, tá deis agam anois cabhrú leis an gcéad ghlúin eile de chraoltóirí óga tairbhe a bhaint as an stáisiún.

Mar a tharlaíonn le gach eagraíocht dheonach bíonn lagtrá ann ó am go ham. Bhí Raidió na Life á reachtáil ón tús mar Chomharchumann agus sna blianta tosaigh bhí go leor de na scair-shealbhóirí gníomhach sa stáisiún. Le himeacht aimsire d'éirigh craoltóirí as agus tháinig craoltóirí nua chun cinn - rud a bhí go breá. Ach deineadh faillí ó thaobh scairshealbhóirí nua a earcú. Mar sin bhí an líon daoine a bhí ag freastal ar chruinnithe cinnbhliana ag dul i laghad ó bhliain go bliain, agus ba dhaoine iad don chuid is mó nach raibh aon bhaint phraiticiúil acu leis an stáisiún. Bhí a laghaid baint idir an Comharchumann agus an stáisiún, nach raibh a fhios fiú ag na craoltóirí deonacha nua go raibh a leithéid de rud ann agus an Comharchumann!

Le cúpla bliain anuas tá próiseas athnuachana ar bun i Raidió na Life. Tá an Bord Bainistíochta níos gníomhaí in obair an stáisiúin ná mar a bhí le roinnt blianta. Eagraíodh ceardlann measúnachta don chéad uair do chraoltóirí an stáisiún faoi stiúr Mary Owens, agus le maoiniú ó Scéim Thacaíocht Pobail Choimisiún Craoltóireachta na hÉireann (Féach Caibidil 4 agus 11). Tá an-mholadh ag dul don scéim seo de chuid an Choimisiúin. Thug sé spreagadh dár gcraoltóirí éirí níos gníomhaí i reachtáil an stáisiúin. Thóg cuid acu orthu féin cruinnithe sóisialta rialta a eagrú ionas go mbeadh níos mó cumarsáide idir lucht an stáisiúin. Tá feachtas díolta scaireanna seolta agus tá ag éirí linn scairshealbhóirí nua a earcú don stáisiún. Tá súil agam faoin am go mbeidh sé seo á léamh go mbeidh cuid de na scairshealbhóirí nua sin ar Bhord Bainistíochta an stáisiúin.

Tá an caibidil seo bunaithe ar mo thaithí pearsanta féin de Raidió na Life, agus tá sé claonta agus easnamhach dá bharr, go háirithe ó thaobh aitheantas a thabhairt do go leor daoine a rinne éacht oibre don stáisiún. Ní rabhas ann mar shampla nuair a bhí an streachailt ar siúl ag dream beag daoine físiúla chun an stáisiún a bhunú. Daoine ar nós Máirín Nic Eoin, Seosamh Ó Murchú, Éamon Ó Dónaill, Máire Ní Chualáin agus Rosemary Day, eagarthóir an leabhair seo. Tá na daoine sin ar fad ag treabhadh goirt úra anois. Tá súil agam go mbeidh siad ag faire go bródúil ar dul chun cinn Raidió na Life sna blianta amach romhainn.

15

Dialogue Not Monologue: Connemara Community Radio

Mary Ruddy and Pat Walshe

Never Mind the Size, It's the Frequency: 87.8 and 106.1 Fm

Mary Ruddy

On 1 July 1995 Connemara Community Radio (CCR) went on air as a licensed community radio station. It was the beginning of a new phase in a project that was itself almost a decade in existence. The story of CCR covers nearly two decades of development. The first ten years, while decidedly more frustrating, were nonetheless significant in shaping the station that went on air in 1995.

When CCR was launched on the airwaves on that Saturday in July 1995, the opening was performed by the grand-daughter of Marconi, Princess Electra. She was in the area at the time at the invitation of the Clifden Chamber of Commerce to mark the 100th anniversary of broadcasting. Guglielmo Marconi, the pioneering engineer credited with inventing radio, had established two stations in North Connemara – a receiver in Currywongan near Letterfrack and a transmitter in Derrygimbla, between Clifden and Ballyconneely. The symbolism of Princess Electra's attendance was not lost on those present. We were a fledgling station pioneering our own new form of radio – albeit on a more modest level. Unlike Marconi, we were exploring new forms of organisation and programme content rather than technology.

While it was a pioneering broadcasting venture for us in Connemara, this model of community broadcasting was already well-established and familiar in parts of northern Europe, Canada, Australia, the United States and South America. We were to some extent re-inventing the wheel only to discover that a form of radio which had a well-grounded philosophy and practice already existed for many decades. Known variously as free radio, associative radio or community radio, they shared a commitment to participative democracy, universal access and innovative programming. This dovetailed elegantly into our own understanding of what we wanted to do and how we wanted to do it. Our understanding of how we would operate a radio service was very much based in community development theory and practice. Community development with its focus on participation, empowerment, and the locality or community as the potential base for social change and action, provided us with a rationale for our new undertaking (see Chapter 5).

In the years prior to going on air we had the opportunity to learn much from individual stations and from AMARC, the international movement for community radio, as well as from the Irish network, the National Association for Community Broadcasting (NACB) and especially from Bray Local Broadcasting (BLB).

In late 1988 we broadcast as a pirate community radio to North Connemara for a brief period, approximately two months. Like virtually all the many other pirate stations, commercial, community and other, we ceased broadcasting at midnight on 30 December 1987. The then Minister for Communications, Ray Burke, had introduced the long-promised legislation permitting licensing of independent stations. The legislation simultaneously introduced severe penalties for stations broadcasting without a licence and, most notably, penalties on anyone placing advertisements with such stations. Overnight, Minister Burke cleared the airwaves making way for an orderly introduction of a new broadcasting environment.

In Connemara we were certainly unhappy that legislation which had been in the pipeline for so long, should be introduced so soon after we finally got on air. However, we consoled ourselves that the preparation for, and the brief experience of operating a radio station, had provided valuable learning and left us poised to obtain a licence to enable us to operate officially and to plan for long-term development. That initial experiment had given us confidence that there was significant community support – both in terms of volunteers and listeners. I recall one letter we received shortly after going off air. It stated: "For the first time I feel that I am living in the centre of where things happen – before the radio brought us our own news, I believed things only happened elsewhere, never here." That alone seemed to make all our efforts worthwhile and we were eager to get back on-air permanently.

Prior to going on air in 1988, it had been my task as an employee of an EU-funded Anti-Poverty project sponsored by Connemara West Plc, a local development company, to research various options for the establishment of a radio station. The term "community radio" was not one we were even familiar with at that time. While researching studio equipment options, I was fortunate enough to be put in contact with Bray Local Broadcasting (BLB) station. While we got very useful and invaluable advice from BLB on technical questions, it was the organisation of BLB that proved most influential. It was there, for the first time, that we encountered the term "community radio". Furthermore, we discovered that there was a well-developed theory and philosophy of community radio, and indeed a worldwide movement, dedicated to the development and promotion of this form of broadcasting. It was a form of organisation and a method of working with which we were immediately comfortable and we believed it paralleled the familiar community development model.

When we went on air in 1988, we had a core of approximately 30 volunteers. We broadcast for two hours every evening and met every Sunday morning to review the previous week's programming and to plan for the following seven days. It was exhilarating. We were learning fast. We were getting a very generous response from listeners.

Our optimism during 1989, that we would soon be back on air, was short-lived when the IRTC announced a three-phase licensing process, commencing with a national station, followed by the county stations, and finally the community and smaller stations. We opposed this at the time, believing that the pressure from the public was not for a national service, but for more local broadcasting, however, our voice was insignificant. With revelations which have since emerged about the role of the then Minister for Communications with the applicants for the ultimately ill-fated, national station, Century Radio, we were clearly not in any position to compete. However, our fate became even more linked with the collapse of "the flagship of Irish broadcasting" as Century Radio had been hailed by the Minister at its launch. Its collapse made the commercial county stations very nervous about financial viability as it did the licensing authority, then the IRTC. The commercial stations successfully convinced the IRTC that to issue any further licences would undermine existing stations. The argument was made, and accepted by the IRTC, that community stations would diminish "their" audience and hence their income from advertising. We battled for seven years to win a licence and only succeeded when there was a change in government which led to a subsequent change in the Board and in the policy of the IRTC.

When the next minister with responsibility for broadcasting, Michael D. Higgins, launched CCR, he launched a station that broadcast for three hours per day, it had one studio in a four-room upstairs space provided rent-free by Connemara West Plc. We had one frequency, 106.8 Fm, which only partially covered the area of North West Connemara for which we held the licence. The area for which we sought and were granted a licence was a contained area, with a strong sense of identity and community – bordering Mayo to the north, the Atlantic to the west, the Twelve Bens to the east and the Connemara Gaeltacht to the south. It is also, in community radio terms, a relatively large geographical area of some 300 square miles (circa 800 square kilometres) but with a small population base of approximately 9,000 people. Indeed this area has one of the lowest population densities in Europe at 11 persons per square kilometre, compared to the European average of 143 and the national average of 51. The main population centre is Clifden town, with a population of just under 1,000. The radio area also covers two islands: Inishbofin (circa 300 persons) and Inishturk (circa 90 persons). The dispersed and rugged terrain did present us with significant technical challenges. One technician on looking at the proposed area for transmission suggested we get a satellite!

Despite being an identifiable community, North Connemara did not have any single development which involved the whole region. CCR presented the first such opportunity. In the pirate phase, community councils in the seven distinct communities were invited to participate in the work of the board of the radio by nominating a representative. When it came to establishing a management board to apply for a licence it was recognised that this was not the preferred model as it tended to encourage a group of individuals who represented seven constituencies rather than nurture a shared responsibility for a single project. On an interim basis, until such time as a legal structure was put in place, it was decided to select individuals who had previously been involved and who had remained with the project through the barren years from 1989 to 1995. Once the station was licensed and operating, a more democratic management structure would be developed.

The initial capital of approximately €32,000 (£25,000) required to bring the skeletal broadcasting equipment from the pirate days up to standard was given by way of an interest-free loan by Connemara West Plc. While the station was an independent project, it was indebted to Connemara West for premises, financial support and for organisational and logistical back-up and support. In return for this, Connemara West would seek and be granted 51 per cent of the ownership of the station as well as the right to nominate two of the seven members of the board of management, including the chairperson. In the ten years since 1995 there have been four chairpersons of CCR, all of whom have been Con West directors or staff members. The remaining membership of the board of management of CCR is composed of two volunteer representatives; two members' representatives; one workers' representative and a representative of Forum, the locally-based rural development company.

The programming hours expanded quite rapidly from our original three hours per day in 1995, until 1999, when they were extended to their present-day duration of ten hours per day. Four of these hours are repeat broadcasts. Today, the station comes on air at 11.00 a.m. and remains on until 9.00 p.m. The programmes that are broadcast between 5.00 pm and 9.00 pm are repeated the following day between noon and 4.00 pm. The first hour, from 11.00 am to 12.00 noon, is live and has a magazine format. The 4.00 pm to 5.00 pm hour, known as *The Gateway Hour*, is reserved for newcomers or others who are not given the imposition of meeting the speech content that applies to others – those are exclusively music programmes.

The programming schedule expanded for a couple of reasons. The primary one being that we were in the happy position of having more volunteers than could be accommodated in the shorter schedule. The second reason was that we were very aware that we were not now in the same broadcasting environment as we were in when we first went on air in 1988. We felt it necessary to ensure that listeners didn't have to keep moving from station to station because we had no service for most of the day. In 1988 we were sharing the airwaves with RTÉ stations only. We were the only broadcaster offering a local service in that area. Seven years later, that space was taken by Galway Bay and, even more, so by Mayo's Mid-West whose signal and type of programming was well received in the area. We were left in the unhappy position of trying to woo listeners away from stations which were much better resourced, more firmly established and to which listeners had already built loyalty.

There are many aspects of the "years in the cold" – 1989 to 1995 – which are regrettable but none, to my mind, as damaging long term as the fact that we had lost listeners whom we would never regain because their requirement for local news and local programming was being satisfied by the commercial county stations. It wasn't only that they had a head-start on the community stations. They were in a position to produce a greater variety of programmes, to a standard and format familiar to listeners and to carry current affairs and news. On that playing field the community stations could not compete. Had we started together, the community stations would have had some opportunity to try to introduce listeners to a new form of radio – it would always have been challenging but we could have given it a good shot.

CCR was concentrating on local stories, we were meeting our 40 per cent speech content. Volunteers were managing to cover events and developments, doing outside broadcasts (OBs) taking training, attending meetings. A lot was, and continues to be, demanded of volunteers, as it was of paid workers. Without question, the commitment of staff and volunteers is the most crucial element in the effective working of a community station. Aspects such as organisational structure, station finances, physical infrastructure of studios and transmitters are clearly also essential but, in the event of any of those breaking down or collapsing, they are more readily fixed. The commitment of volunteers and staff is essential and precious. If lost, it is not easily regained.

CCR has had in the region of 100 volunteers since the very early days. New people join, others leave, some have been there from the beginning, others join for intense short periods – all are essential. CCR has been particularly fortunate in the calibre and dedication of the volunteers it has attracted. Prior to going on air in 1995, we were conscious that while the concept of participation is central to community development, it is a challenging and difficult concept to make real in practice. Participation implies significant involvement in all aspects of the station, in programme production, decision making, planning and management. It is clearly insufficient to state that one has "an open door" as it is only those with sufficient confidence who will cross the threshold. It is the experience of most community stations that those who wish to take up the opportunity for self-expression are not the "voiceless" or the "marginalised" but the articulate and opinionated, those already privileged in educational and social terms. The same is true in relation to those seeking a role in the management or planning aspects of a station.

Walter Lippman, a prominent American journalist and critic, was amongst the first to claim that with the emergence of mass media there was a revolution in the art of democracy. He argued that, for the first time, it was possible to manufacture consent, to bring about agreement on the part of the public. Unlike later theorists such as Noam Chomsky, Lippman viewed this as a positive development. Lippman argued that in a democracy there are two classes of citizens – the small, specialised class active in decision-making, governing, analysing and the large majority, "the bewildered herd", who are passive spectators. Lenin's notion of "the vanguard" and "the masses" posited the same thinking from the other end of the political spectrum.

In CCR we did try consciously and consistently to avoid being a station of the élites or the vanguards only. In trying to ensure widespread participation, CCR, in common with very many other community stations, provides training, free of charge, to individuals. Initially, this training was provided by way of general invitation with the clear expectation that those who participated would go on to volunteer to work in some capacity in the station. This worked well in getting many individuals interested and competent to work as technicians, programme-makers, presenters, etc. However, it was insufficient on its own to ensure the participation of certain sectors of the community. While the station has generally been happy with the numerical participation of women in the station, it was conscious that women were not as highly represented in the technical and sporting areas, traditionally perceived as more appropriate to males. To address this, CCR, in conjunction with the National University of Ireland, Galway (NUI, Galway), developed a proposal to run intensive training for women in all areas of media including theory and practice as well as raising awareness about the gender dimension implicit in all broadcasting. The IRTC also came on board as a partner in the project, which became known as "Women-on-Air". It was largely funded by the EU under the New Opportunities for Women (NOW) programme with significant financial support from the IRTC and support in kind from NUI, Galway and CCR. The training ran for four years; initially training was delivered in Letterfrack using CCR's premises and subsequently it moved to Galway city when the training was opened out to women throughout the west of Ireland.

The age profile of volunteers was another source of concern in that the bulk were aged between 30-50 years. Young people and those of 60+ years were under-represented. To redress the imbalance of younger people, the station worked with Transition Year students in the local community school and with Youthreach and Youth in Action projects. The involvement of older people was stimulated through initiatives with Active Age groups but in general their involvement remains primarily in their being the station's most loyal listeners.

In addition to the transmission problems posed by the large geographic area encompassed by the station, it also posed problems of access for volunteers. Getting to a studio was and continues to be a barrier to participation. We noted early on that the levels of participation decreased as one moved in a concentric circle away from the studio premises in Letterfrack. Most volunteers came from within a five-mile radius of the studio. This difficulty was further exacerbated for those living on the two populated islands within our area. To address the difficulty the station began to look at the feasibility of additional studios. In December 1998, CCR launched a mobile radio unit to be based in Clifden pending the opening of a permanent studio in the town. This mobile unit, which was an old traveling bank, was to be based in Clifden but would also be available for outside broadcasts. However, as Pat Walshe describes below, its life was short-lived, as problems with the vehicle itself and the cost of insurance rendered it economically unviable. With some greater success, the station launched an on-air studio on Inishbofin island in 2000. This was a joint effort between the island's own community group who undertook to provide premises and to cover current costs while CCR were responsible for the equipping of the studio and the provision of training and organisational support. This shared responsibility for the studio proved a useful strategy and reflected the community development approach employed by CCR.

Without overstating the case, it is a challenge for a newly formed community station to try to accommodate "the community" – the masses and the vanguard, the specialists and the generalists. It is all too easy, and potentially rewarding in financial and listenership terms, to become a cosy station, unchallenging and cautious in its programming, reassuring to its listeners with popular and acceptable formats and content. Of course, at the other extreme, it can become a station which unsympathetically probes, harangues and provokes its listeners, perhaps from a fixed ideological perspective, as has been the experience with some of the more radical European stations. The challenge of a community station is to seek dialogue, not monologue, which can accommodate the popular reassuring type programme as well as take on the marginal, the challenging and the uncomfortable. The ultimate aim for a community station is to be the authentic voice, not *for* the community, but *of* the community.

During the "cold years" while the radio board continued to meet, to explore other options, to lobby and plan to get back on air, a training course supported by FÁS (who operate the Government Community Employment (CE) Scheme) was organised and, under the supervision of a local archaeologist, the trainees started to record recollections of older members of the community with a view to making radio programmes for the station. In the absence of the radio, it was ultimately decided to publish the material in book form. This very attractive publication, *Hidden Connemara*, was launched with a preface by Noel Browne, former Minister for Health. While much of the recollections were nostalgic memories of items such as herbal and folk remedies, working on the bog and school days long ago, a section dealt with childbirth and memories of untold hurt and grief emerged on the practice of burying unbaptised, stillborn children in unconsecrated ground. Parents who had lost a child, or indeed a number of children, spoke of the pain of seeing the ground in which their children were buried left unmarked and in some cases being eroded by the sea. This led to a ceremony performed by the Catholic Church where the children's remains were re-interred in the local cemetery and the parents were much comforted by the public recognition of their loss. A striking change from the secret, almost shameful, experience of burying their child quietly and unceremoniously during the 1930s, '40s and even later.

That experience reinforced our understanding of the power of making public, or bringing into the public arena, stories and experiences and the potential, albeit limited, to lead to change. *Hidden Connemara* became almost a prototype for how programming on the station would develop. In general, items were innocuous enough – interesting, sometimes nostalgic, popular and appealing but, every now and again, a chord was touched that was uncomfortable, awkward, unpopular. Located in the context of a station with which the vast majority of the community felt ownership, such a programme was all the more powerful and could lead to its being heard in a way that a station viewed as unsympathetic or uninformed about the area could not.

In dealing with charged issues on CCR, the station deliberately moved away from the confrontational debate format which presented conflicting and contrary opinions. Fish-farming was a highly controversial topic in the area during the early years of the station's life. It would not have been difficult to produce programmes which would have been heated and highly argumentative. The station chose instead to try to look at the various arguments and engaged, only occasionally, those in the frontline. CCR sought instead to clarify the issues and to add some factual information to the debate, so that listeners were better equipped to make informed decisions. In short, we tried to bring light rather than heat to a subject which had all the potential to lead to bitter and enduring division in the community. We were certainly not in the business of making "entertainment" out of this topic, despite the ease with which that could have been done and, no doubt, the station would have been rewarded with increased listenership.

Community radio is not just local radio on a smaller scale – it is a different form of broadcasting. It is different in organisation, in rationale, in history and, most importantly, it is different in its relationship to the community of which it is a part. But such a form of radio creates many challenges. How does one resolve the dilemma between demanding high standards in programming and encouraging wide participation? Of course, those of us committed to radio and broadcasting also need to appreciate that not everybody is, or wants to be, either a broadcaster or involved in organised community activities. The challenge is to ensure that those who do are facilitated and actively encouraged.

Reflecting on more than ten years plus of community broadcasting in Ireland, there are a number of issues which appear critical to how community broadcasting can continue to develop. Community radio in Ireland began and continues in a period of great change and uncertainty for broadcasting generally as we moved away from the traditional public service monopoly to a competitive, market-led, deregulated arena. This arena is not hospitable to community broadcasting, or to any small-scale operation, as is being witnessed by the ever increasing pressure on freeing up restrictions on ownership and on increasing market size. Community radio faces a significant pressure to find and to hold its place in the broadcasting landscape. Competing with commercial and public service radio stations by providing, or attempting to provide, similar programming is not a viable option. However, while community radio does not occupy centre-stage in the broadcasting landscape, this does not mean it should confine itself to a marginal and residual space – operating only where it is commercially unattractive or confining itself only to the most marginal programming. Community radio needs the confidence to create its own broadcasting space and to avoid becoming a poor caricature of "big" radio.

The new competitive environment of the twenty-first century may lead to increased station choice but, as anyone who has spent time cruising the spectrum will report, this has not led to increased programming choice. An IRTC conference once borrowed a phrase from Bruce Springsteen to give a name to this phenomenon: "57 Channels and Nothing On". Programming is ultimately what radio is about. Of course, the organisation of the station, the management and the technology are all vital, but at the end of the day any station will be judged by the quality of its programme content – or it should be. Yet if we look at the measurements that are employed by broadcasters, the Joint National Listenership Research (JNLR) surveys conducted quarterly – what do they tell us about the quality, innovativeness, creativity of programming? Nothing! They tell us the audience figures for stations and for shows on those stations. They are conducted for the advertising agencies. But is this what radio is about? Perhaps for the hard-nosed business person it is, but it does not provide the rationale for those committed to community broadcasting. However, this should not lead to a dismissal of audience size. There is a position argued within the community radio sector which tends to disregard audience size. I believe this is misplaced, but it does bring us around to the question: To whom does community radio owe a duty? Is it to volunteers, to listeners, to the wider community? My position is that community radio owes a duty to all of these. Furthermore, as a user of a public resource, the airwaves, it has a further duty to ensure that this resource is used effectively and efficiently to the benefit of the wider community. However, this does not necessarily mean that one goes for the highest possible numbers at all times; a community station should seek to address and appeal to all sectors of the community, at some time, over a weekly programme schedule.

Outside Broadcasts by Connemara Community Radio

Pat Walshe

As we travelled west, back from Sherries on a Saturday evening, after completing our last outside broadcast of the 2005 AIL rugby season, I was reflecting on CRC's upcoming tenth birthday and the part outside broadcasts had played in its development. I suppose the geographic location of CCR had a lot to do with the fact that we had an outside broadcast unit (OBU) before we had a licence. This I confirmed from a label on our first, and still functioning OBU, the date 16/10/94 was written on a stick-on label pasted on the unit almost a year before we went on air.

The unit is a Professional 10-channel slim type MX 10 Series stereo audio mixer, made in the USA, and it cost the equivalent of €1,000. That was a lot of money at the time. However, it was used last week to do a broadcast from the Community Centre in Maam and the quality is as good today as the first day when we embarked, in our innocence, on our first outside broadcast. The main reason we felt the necessity to be able to do outside broadcasts, all those years ago, was because of the large geographic area, around 800 square kilometres, which is North West Connemara. So outside broadcasting was born.

At first, we covered activities like regattas, pony shows, arts festivals and this was followed by programmes from various community groups like community councils, women's groups, Irish nights. There were a lot of requests for regular broadcasts of mass which is very important to those in the population who are elderly and not mobile. At first we were only able to broadcast midnight Mass and special services from the Church of Ireland on occasions like Christmas Eve. However, now we are able to broadcast mass weekly from Clifden, which is greatly appreciated, especially by the housebound. Requests also came in to cover the welcoming home celebrations of winners of national awards like the gold medal winners in Fleadh Ceoil na hÉireann or the All Ireland Handball winners or the Connemara Blacks, winners of the AIL Division 3.

However, the biggest development for CCR has been the live coverage of sports event and, in particular, broadcasting live rugby matches. CCR has travelled to all four provinces in the land over the last three years covering the away matches of the local rugby team, the Connemara Blacks. This has a huge effect on the way our listeners think about CCR. We are the only station to cover these games and it has added to the profile of community radio and generated further goodwill and appreciation among the community. The credibility, quality and reliability of this go-anywhere radio is acknowledged on match programmes and in pre-match speeches and indeed, on the touchline, when people approach the unit to enquire about community radio and are amazed by the concept.

The technology we use is straightforward enough – we have a "reporta phone" which is connected to the studio via a mobile phone. As the years have gone by the quality has greatly improved as networks improved and so has our own expertise. At one stage we broadcast a match, recorded it in the studio and burnt off copies on CD and sold them.

There are many stories about outside broadcasts, like the time we were in the village of Cleggan. The nearest phone was 200 metres from the community centre so we ran a line from the nearest house to the community centre across a field. All was going well until someone rushed in to say that some cows were examining the telephone line and were going to eat it. The broadcast continued with a volunteer bravely guarding the telephone line for the duration of the programme. Another time we went to Maam to broadcast Mass. We were to connect to the phone line in the local medical dispensary but, when we arrived the dispensary was shut, so we had to climb the nearest telephone pole to connect for the broadcast. Needless to say this is not recommended to other aspiring community radio broadcasters but sometimes the show must go on.

At the moment we do approximately 100 outside broadcasts in the year. This brings the smaller communities within North West Connemara to the fore and gives them the opportunity to be heard. It also brings services to the community that are not provided by any other source. Outside broadcasting has been a very important part of the development of CCR in its lifetime. It has become part of every day life for large numbers of people and has helped with community development in our area. For people to hear items like the Sunday Mass coming from their own parish church, it has added another community to the radio station, or in a way, community radio has reconnected these people to their community

From the beginning, there were some extra challenges for CCR in its endeavours to serve its franchise area. As well as the usual start-up problems that all community radio stations experience, there was the additional challenge of the Connemara landscape, with the Twelve Bens and the Maamturk mountains on the east side and the Atlantic on the west and the offshore Islands of Inishbofin and Inishturk. Inishbofin island is three miles long and one and a half miles wide with less than 300 inhabitants and is located nine miles northwest of Cleggan, and Inishturk, a smaller island with a population of 93, is a two-hour trip from Cleggan.

The CCR crew en mass make an annual visit to Inishbofin and have done so from our earliest days. These visits by the radio were an attempt to include the people of the island in the activities of the radio and also to give them the opportunity to participate in the activities of the extended Connemara community by forging links with the mainland using radio as a bridge. It was also seen as an opportunity for Inishbofin to share its history and culture with the broader community, most of whom, strangely enough, had never been to the island. These trips were eagerly looked forward to by both the volunteers from CCR and the islanders.

The first phase of the trip to broadcast on the island was the loading of outside broadcast equipment in the cars at the station in Letterfrack. This was done in a military fashion. As each item was checked off as it was loaded up there was no room for error, for once we landed on the island we couldn't come back for a vital piece of equipment. On arrival at the pier in Cleggan, the first thing was a quick glance in the direction of the sea. Would it be a pleasant trip or would we have to ride the waves? Whatever the conditions at sea, we had to get on with the task of loading the outside broadcast equipment on board with the assistance of Paul

O'Halloran, grandson of the Skipper, Paddy O'Halloran, who has run the mail boat to and from the island since the service was provided by a sail boat. You always felt reassured with a man of Paddy's experience at the helm as he would only travel if it was safe to do so. Once the equipment was safely on board, it was covered to protect it from possible rain or a wave that might just wash over the deck.

The trip was nearly always good while the boat was in Cleggan Bay. If we were going to have rough patch it would be when we left the shelter of the bay and met the Atlantic and turned north for the island. When we arrived in Inishbofin Bay the boat would anchor off-shore as the water was too shallow to allow the large boat to dock at the pier. We would be ferried the rest of the way to the island by currach which would be loaded until the water was an inch from the top of the boat. On arrival at the beach, the boat man would jump out and pull the currach on to the sand, and some of the cargo would be removed to allow the passengers to go ashore. Bit by bit the outside broadcast equipment would be on loaded and transferred to what ever transport was available on the day – a pickup truck, an old Eircom Renault Van with no door on the passenger side or, at a later stage, a quad bike. Sometimes this transfer would give rise for concern about the safety of the equipment, first because of the water and second because of rough handling.

The equipment would be delivered to the selected location, either Murray's Hotel or Day's Hotel or maybe Day's pub or the island's national school. The next concern was the telephone line which provided our link to the mainland – where the line was located and how we would get it from our location were important considerations as our limits were a 200 metre roll of cable. On rare occasions this would be extended to the last but mostly the line would be in the same building and our 20-metre length of telephone cable would be carefully strung across the bar or dining room to the broadcast equipment. The tense time was at the test stage when the equipment was all connected and the line was connected to the interface with the desk, then a call would be put through to the studio in Letterfrack. Once we had confirmed that we had a clear telephone line back to the studio technician, the next step was to link to the desk and check the levels from each microphone around the makeshift studio in Inishbofin. Then, and only then, with everything tested, could we finally relax.

A trip to the pub for a bite to eat was the next priority, now that the tummy had settled after the sea crossing and the equipment was all set and ready to go. The pub, of course, was a good place to meet old acquaintances and to get a feel for what was happening on the island. Local musicians were usually to be found in sessions with their own unique style of traditional music blended with a hint of the influence of musicians who have visited the island down through the years. We would invite them to the OBU where they would play or sing between interviews. Like true professionals they would start to play as the interview came to an end and the next interview was being organised. It never ceased to amaze me how quickly they instinctively knew their role as providers of continuity links between interviews, as well as their role as musicians. It was on an occasion such as this that we first met Dessie O'Halloran of "Say you love me" fame. Dessie was asked if he listened to CCR and he replied, "Aren't I killed from turning ye off!" To this day CCR claims responsibility for the fame Dessie later achieved.

On these trips we sometimes stayed over and enjoyed the great hospitality of the people of Inishbofin and the music of the Inishbofin Céilí Band and other local musicians and singers. These sessions were particularly enjoyable when the sea was rough and you knew that you were in a nice place, with a warm fire and good company – somehow you appreciate life much more when you are closer to nature and the elements.

As well as locals there were always people from all parts of the world who came to Inishbofin for a holiday and years later are still there because of the wonderful lifestyle that the island offers. As time went by CCR and the people of the island felt it was time to establish a studio there and made media history in 2000 with the official opening of Ireland's first island radio studio on In-ishbofin. With initial funding in 1996 from the Ireland Fund, CCR had commenced training with volunteers from Inishbofin island. This led to demand for opportunities for more direct involve-ment. The Inishbofin Development Committee gave a free space in the Community Centre for the setting up of a studio facility and with a grant of approximately €20,000 from the Department of Arts, Culture, Gaeltacht and the Islands for equipment, the stu-dio was set up with full ISDN connection enabling direct broad-casting from the Inishbofin community. Today, a weekly, hour-long programme is broadcast from the Inishbofin studio on Wednesdays from 5.00 pm to 6.00 pm.

Inishbofin Arts week in May is now the excuse for the annual trip to Inishbofin for the volunteers from the mainland. This yearly event is keenly looked forward to as it gives a chance to meet the volunteers from the island again and to the share in the hospitality and the craic. Our hopes for the future for community radio on Inishbofin is to increase the hours of broadcasting from the island and in particular to look at a weekend programme that would involve the youth of the island, who are away at boarding school during the week.

Inishturk Island, which is in Mayo, has a lot of interaction with Inishbofin and Renvyle. The mail boat to Inishturk went from Renvyle until relatively recently. The people of Inishturk take part in outside broadcasts from Inishbofin and are regular contributors to CCR through programmes such as *Community Matters* on Tuesdays and *The Great Outdoors* on Thursdays. The people of Clare Island, Inishturk and CCR are all enthusiastic about the fu-ture of community radio on the islands and look forward to link-ing up more closely in the future.

In 1997, the Clifden branch of the Bank of Ireland contacted us to say they were replacing their travelling bank unit and the old one would be available to us to convert to an outside broadcasting studio, if we wished. After some consideration we decided to go ahead with this project. We converted the truck into a studio and painted it with the Connemara Community Radio logo. It looked great and the future possibilities for outside broadcasts appeared limitless. The next step, however, gave us a clue that this project may not be the best idea we ever had. We had to get road tax and Insurance for the truck and the drivers needed to have C licences to drive a heavy goods vehicle. In true CCR fashion, all these problems were overcome and the show got on the road. There were many uses for the new outside broadcast unit: it could be parked in Clifden and act as a studio, or it could travel from village to village to do programmes and this it did for a while.

However, we discovered there were limitations. As it needed to be connected to a power supply and a telephone line, it could not go off-road to cover sporting events and on one occasion in Clifden, when the power was connected, the desk became alive. This was caused by a leak in the roof and water had made its way on to the equipment. On one of its first "road trips" the engine gave up the ghost. This brought to an end the very short life of the Bank of Ireland OBU. In 2004, when Bank of Ireland withdrew the travelling bank service from the Connemara area, they again kindly offered us their unit, but after our previous experience we declined. At the moment we have a converted trailer which we use for the Clifden Pony Show. The conversion was done by a Youth Reach project in Letterfrack. Sporting events like rugby and GAA matches are done from the sideline and all other outside broadcasts are done on site, courtesy of the host.

The support and assistance of the public in supplying power, telephone lines and premises to do broadcasts over the years has been great. We have never had a refusal in ten years. While you might expect that type of support in your own area, we have had the same experience in venues big and small all around the country. Community radio is well-respected and supported all over Ireland.

For Connemara Community Radio outside broadcasting has been a important contributing factor to our success as it has provided access for people all over a large franchise area, and now these people see the radio as being theirs.

16

Agitate, Educate, Organise: Dundalk Fm 100

Alan Byrne

When the parameters of your life change and you get a glimpse of a different future, this becomes your vision. For me, one of those moments happened in the Seagoe Hotel, Portadown in April 2001. Three hundred teenagers from secondary schools in Northern Ireland and the six border counties of the Republic assembled to make presentations about tourism interests in their areas. Two groups, one from Bundoran and a second from East Belfast, had edited short video/slideshow presentations. Watching the pupils react to seeing themselves and their areas on the big screen gave me the impression that this was really an exercise in confident self-expression – a chance to reflect their identity.

In the afternoon workshop, we tried to script and record a radio ad for some local tourist attractions. Using the primitive Windows sound recorder function on the office computer, a cheap plastic microphone and a stereo to play background music we succeeded in making some fairly interesting promos. As I drove home, I thought that if the students had so many ideas to share, then maybe it was time that people where I came from were ready to talk publicly about the Troubles and how they had made a difference to their lives. It was time to start a radio station.

Back in the office, I searched the internet for "Community Media Ireland". I located a budget film-making course in the Nerve Centre in Derry. The Spence Brothers from Comber in Co. Down were facilitating the course. The weekend cost £10 sterling and was a priceless introduction to the world of video making. That night, having settled in a bed and breakfast close to the city centre, I listened in to *McClain's Country* on BBC Radio Foyle – local accents talking about lyrics, songs and influences. The TV was tuned to Channel 9, Derry's own community TV channel which was running ads for sports shops and record stores while playing music videos and requests for young lovers and their friends.

In June 2001, knowing I was soon to be unemployed, I was sitting in the kitchen with a notebook scribbling ideas as they entered my head: Dundalk Community Media Centre – Stage 1, set up a local community radio followed by Stage 2, find out if there was enough support for a local community TV.

It was a great excuse to travel around Ireland and meet people who were working in community radio and film centres. Ciarán Kissane at the BCI recommended a trip to Kilkee for the first Community Radio Training Féile (see Chapters 4 and 11). There, over a weekend, I met most of the people who became influential in shaping the concept of community radio and community development through radio, as the Dundalk Media Centre grew from an idea into a reality. But before that could happen there was some groundwork to do, some more people to meet: Connemara Community Radio (CCR, see Chapter 15) Community Radio Castlebar (CCR, see Chapter 8), the Galway Film Centre, the Cork Film Centre, Community Radio Youghal (CRY, see Chapter 12), the Nerve Centre in Derry, Northern Visions in Belfast, NEAR Fm (see Chapters 2, 6 and 7) operating on the northside of Dublin, Tallaght Community Radio (TCR) operating on the rooftop of the Tallaght Shopping Centre and the Community Media Network (CMN), who were operating out of top floor offices on Parnell Square in Dublin.

In Letterfrack, Linda and Gráinne O'Malley introduced me to CCR. You cannot but be impressed when you hear they have three studios, including one on the island of InishBofin. They told me how Connemara West Plc, a local development company, had backed their idea. If everyone in their community tuned in at the same time, they would have 10,000 listeners. They were proud of their "Wall of Sound" – VHS tape recordings of everything that had been broadcast since day one. Ten years later they were still recording each day's broadcast to VHS. I imagined that one day a summer student would have the job of digitising that wonderful archive. How many hours of broadcasting would that be? I returned to Letterfrack when the Community Radio Training Féile was held there in 2003.

I remember walking in to the Tallaght Shopping Centre and looking for Tallaght Community Radio (TCR). Declan McLoughlin, then the TCR station manager and now working with the BCI, told me about his job and explained the technical side of things to me. He showed me the studios and explained how their advertising and programme promos were recorded and played out.

At the studio at Community Radio Youghal (CRY), I remember chatting to the volunteers over a cup of coffee and a cigarette. CRY had rent-free premises and were using software to play out programmes. A skinhead girl was presenting a Saturday morning women's hour – it was all exciting and possible.

Through a voyage of exploration around the island of Ireland, I discovered the world of community media. It is a place where many diverse groups and individuals combine their talents in an effort to agitate for change – people who want to democratise the media. It can be done through community radio giving access to and training in radio skills. Slowly, all over the country, people who were receiving training as sound-desk operators, researchers, editors and presenters were blossoming into a community movement of their own.

There are so many impressions imprinted on my mind from those visits but one that stands out more than any was the "Refugee Week" that NEAR Fm devoted to immigrants living in their community. All of the programmes during this week were presented by people from other countries. I still cannot imagine someone from Congo presenting the Dundalk Fm Sunday morning show *Magic Moments* asking people to remember the dancing to the 1960s showbands at the Pavillion, The Adelphi and courting in the kitchen, but you never know. I particularly admired NEAR Fm's policy of educating their listeners, a conscious policy by a conscientious station.

With the assistance of the FÁS Social Economy Programme, the Dundalk Media Centre was incorporated in January 2002. With the support and guidance of the founding members who formed the first Board of Directors and the enthusiasm and friendliness of the staff that were employed, we gave the impression that the Media Centre was an exciting addition to the town of Dundalk. Our mission was to bring in as many community groups for interview as we could and hope they would like what they saw and be encouraged to start a programme of their own.

We settled into an upstairs office in the centre of town belonging to the Dundalk Employment Partnership. I remember sitting in a green office which was being used as a storeroom. Apart from the furniture, I had a notepad and a pen. On the floor were white sheets of paper marking out where the radio studio, video editing suite, news room and manager's office would be located. The partitions went up and the rooms were painted, the radio studio, no bigger than a box room, had blue carpet on the floor and on the walls. It contained two mini-disc players, two CD players, a double tape deck, a headphone distributor, a sound desk, a compressor and a record deck – end of story. The presenter faced into the wall, while to the side we could fit in up to three guests. We were linked to our transmitter in the Hotel Imperial through ISDN lines. The office was often thronged with people working, recording, teaching, editing, some people visiting and some on business. There really was no room for hanging around. We always had one or two young people in on work experience.

We applied for and were granted a temporary licence which gave us a chance to test out our ideas and ourselves. The first day's broadcast was going according to plan. Most shows had been recorded and edited on to individual mini-disks. Our first live show was between 1.00 pm and 2.00 pm on a Saturday lunchtime. The concept was simple – bring in a musician for a live half hour set; it seemed like a great way to showcase local talent. Jinx Lennon and Deirdre Keelan arrived with a guitar, an amplifier and a keyboard. Our first phone call came from a woman called Valerie who lambasted us for playing pro-IRA music on the radio. Jinx sang songs about kids joyriding, drinking in fields, conflict between gangs and the way Dundalk's name had been lowered because of the black market and IRA links. He also wrote some love songs. I quickly realised that when you are communicating with so many different types of listener, the message sent out does not always end up as the message received.

I brought the staff on a visit to Virgin Fm in London. The young manager there spoke of his community radio days when everybody had to know how to do everything. We had just missed the morning crew, but the studio was filled with the smell of stale cigarettes, empty coffee cups and sandwich wrappers. The mike was suspended from the ceiling as the DJs liked to move around and one presenter was even hooked up to a radio mike. We were told that in the case of a security alert, Virgin Radio could continue to broadcast from a number of different studios throughout the city. This started me thinking about all those "What ifs": What if the electricity cuts out? What if the transmitter breaks down? What if terrorists take over the studio?

With the assistance of Peace and Reconciliation funding, we relocated to larger premises in the same complex in April 2004. Six months later, we signed a five-year contract with the BCI. On 15 September 2004, Dundalk Fm 100 commenced broadcasting from 9.00 am to 1.00 pm on Monday to Friday and from 9.00 am to midnight on Saturday and Sunday. The build-up of experience of our weekend presenters meant that they continued on from where they had left off nearly one year previously when our pilot licence expired. Four years later, 60 per cent of the original weekend presenters are still on air. We have 84 shows during 106 hours of broadcasting each week.

In January 2005, five members of the Dundalk and District Summer League organising committee completed a radio course and took on a 90-minute programme covering amateur soccer matches in Dundalk. The passion, knowledge and pace of the programme immediately attracted more than just the core audience of soccer fans. During the programme, the presenters rang for updates to local live matches and suddenly football managers were giving interviews on the touchline and texting in as goals were scored. During the course of the season, listeners came to recognise the managers' voices and to learn a lot about the organisation and the presenters' personalities. As a result, Dundalk Fm installed a phone line in the press box of Oriel Park in time to cover the Summer League's Clancy Cup Final. It was our first live sports broadcast. Now all Dundalk FC home matches are broadcast live. The commentators receive text messages about the game from people in the stand and from fans listening on the internet. This shows that sports coverage is one programme type where community radio could dedicate more airtime and receive immediate response and recognition. It develops two-way communication, real and relevant live programming and builds listener loyalty and identification with *their* community radio station.

17

Northern View:
Inishowen Community Radio

Jim Doherty and Jimmy McBride

Inishowen Community Radio (ICR, *Radió Pobal Inis Eoghain*) began as all community radio stations do: in response to a demand
from the local community. Back in the days when Raidió Éireann
was the only choice on the airwaves, Inishowen, like many parts
of rural Ireland, had a hugely popular pirate station, North West
Community Radio (NWCR), which provided the local community
with its own distinctive voice. Despite its illegal status, NWCR
had a strong community focus and much of its programming was
made by dedicated volunteers. It provided a wide mix of music,
craic and coverage of local events and people. When the first local commercial licences were awarded in the late 1980s, the people behind NWCR and the Inishowen community it served were
extremely disappointed when the local licence went elsewhere ...
but that's another story!

Gradually, the Inishowen community came to realise that,
while popular and entertaining, the local commercial station
wasn't catering sufficiently to their specific needs. There was
something lacking, a feeling that in the new licensed, commercial
era something from the old pirate "do-it-yourself" days was missing. And then it finally dawned – the community was missing, or

rather the type of station in which the community was involved as "producers" and not just as "consumers" of radio, the type of station that is community inspired and community controlled. This awareness came at a time when the Inishowen community, reeling from unemployment, emigration and lack of investment in the area, realised that it had to start sorting out its own problems, that community development was both its own responsibility and the best means of addressing its problems. Because of its unique location, geographically the most northerly part of Ireland yet not politically part of Northern Ireland but the Irish Republic, Inishowen had suffered greatly from the war in the North. This legacy of the conflict was massive unemployment and lack of opportunity and development throughout the peninsula.

The original application was submitted by Inishowen Rural Development Limited (IRDL), itself a community owned and controlled local development partnership, working over a range of sectors in the Inishowen region. IRDL people like Michael Heaney, Aideen Doherty and Clare Mulhall were the driving force behind setting up the community station at this time. They could foresee the benefits that a community radio station would bring to the area and the important role that it could play in community development. The growth in community development and demands for action, driven mostly by volunteers and community activists, resulted in meaningful levels of funding becoming available here for the first time. LEADER and European Peace and Reconciliation funding would help to dramatically improve the quality of life for the community here and to provide the essential resources for a new community radio station. The IRTC, as the BCI was then, offered the group a licence in the summer of 1998, the granting and signing of which was completed in September 2000. ICR came on air on Monday, 13 November 2000.

The community group behind ICR, Raidió Pobal Inis Eoghain, was formed in the autumn of 1998 as an independent stand-alone body after public meetings were held in various locations around the general Inishowen area. Nine representatives from the community were elected to become the board of management. These meetings drew massive attendances and helped to promote the idea of and support for the station throughout Inishowen. Many of those who were elected to the original board, like Jimmy McBride and P.J. McLaughlin, are still heavily involved with ICR. Others, like Hugo Boyce, Eamonn McLaughlin, Dessie McCallion and Brendan Fletcher played an important role in establishing the station and only left the board in recent years. Three representatives from IRDL were nominated to the board. Registration as a limited company was completed and signed in December 1998. The composition of the new board elected after the first AGM was to be as follows: two station employees/volunteers, six community representatives, three nominated IRDL representatives and two nominated representatives from statutory or funding agencies.

The initial set-up costs of the service were grant-assisted by IRDL (through its LEADER 2 Programme), the Programme for Peace and Reconciliation, the Inishowen Partnership, Donegal County Council and by subscriptions from several interested local businesses and individuals. As Jimmy McBride says, the efforts to get the station on-air were not easy:

> Although the board was set up in 1998, it took another two years before we started broadcasting. At times we thought that it would never happen! I remember us having our monthly meetings and wondering if it was ever going to happen. Progress was slow and much of the initial enthusiasm in the community waned. People got fed up asking me "when is the new station going to start?" We had conducted a lot of local fund-raising and people were beginning to wonder what we had done with the money! A lot of volunteers had been trained too and nearly two years later had no station in which to use their new-found skills. That was an awkward time – I think the community, and I would include myself and the Board in this – unrealistically expected progress to be much faster. We were learning that setting up a licensed station was

a much slower process than setting up an illegal one! But we persevered, even while we were having doubts if it would ever happen at all.

There were several reasons for the delay, all of them outside the board's control. Inishowen is a very mountainous region and this proved a nightmare in transmission terms. To cover the area properly required two transmission sites, which increased the set-up costs dramatically, and the planning application process was slow. As McBride explains:

> We had problems in securing all the required sites and funding. While we had more than 50 per cent of it tied down we encountered difficulties in securing the rest. The length of time it took from submitting a funding application until it was granted took ages. Besides, we were all doing this voluntarily and most of us had no experience in this type of thing. It's not every day that you set up a licensed radio station, deal with funding organisations or the IRTC, so we were all on a steep learning curve.

Raidió Pobal Inis Eoghain represents and serves all sections of the community and all sectors are encouraged to become involved as much as possible. One of the central roles of the station is to tackle the problems of social exclusion – those who are marginalised, minorities, whoever and wherever they are in Inishowen are encouraged to get involved with ICR. The ethos of the station is to be as inclusive, representative and supportive of all sections of Inishowen life as possible. The setting up of the station was especially valuable given the isolated location of the region. All involved in the project work unstintingly to achieve the goals of informing, educating and entertaining all of the people of Inishowen, and this is in line with the community radio policies as proposed by the BCI. The station is a focal point for the free expression of diverse opinion and is a channel for showcasing local talent delivering the intelligent and unique perspectives that the community of Inishowen offers. The service offers equality of representation to all groups and provides the necessary skills, through professional training and motivation, to empower all groups to illustrate their talents as effectively as possible.

Once funding was guaranteed, and the first of it became available early in 2000, the board recruited the first ICR staff member. This was P.J. McLaughlin, who was a member of the original board and someone who was well-known locally as "PJ the DJ", a nickname earned from his days on pirate radio in the northwest. McLaughlin was employed through the Jobs Initiative Programme of the Inishowen Partnership and his role was to set up an office for the new station in the IRDL building in Carndonagh. He laughs:

> At that stage my only experience in radio was of the "skull and crossbones" variety but that was all that was available around here. I was always fully committed to the ideals of community radio and desperately wanted to play my part in acquiring an Inishowen station. I would definitely say that I am now totally rehabilitated broadcasting-wise and my pirate days are well behind me!

When Peace and Reconciliation funding came through in spring 2000 the board was finally able to recruit a station manager and the job was offered to a man who had been awaiting just such an opportunity. Jim Doherty, a native of Inishowen with wide experience in media broadcasting, was appointed station manager in May, 2000. He accelerated the slow process encountered by the board and was responsible for expediting the outstanding issues. He was largely instrumental in finally getting the station on air in November 2000. Doherty says:

> I left Inishowen, like so many others, for college in 1982 and was then working in Dublin. I had always dreamed of returning home to live and work and to use whatever skills and experience I had for the benefit of my own community but, until

ICR, there were no suitable opportunities for me. I had been involved in community radio in Dublin with Dublin Weekend Radio and Raidió na Life (see Chapter 14) and also worked in commercial radio but my heart was always in the community sector. The chance to come home and play an instrumental role in establishing a community station in my native place was a dream come true.

The first few months of the new manager's employment were a crazy time ... and it hasn't got much more sane since! Doherty jokes:

It's been a rollercoaster since day one! If I had known then what I know now, I would probably have stayed in Dublin. I've looked at my initial contract and job description several times since and scratch my head. However, each day was and is totally different and the whole experience has been fascinating and worth every minute.

The initial set-up costs were met largely by the original funders. However, the ongoing running of the station was to be funded by initiatives generated by the board and the manager. Since advertising and sponsorship was limited, the manager set about exploring various other funding agencies which would be prepared to participate in initiatives and programmes that would be in keeping with the ethos of the station. For the first year Doherty and McLaughlin were the only paid staff at the station, which was totally reliant on the commitment and efforts of its dedicated team of volunteers. Some of those first volunteers are still fully involved with the station. People like Mickey Donaghey, Adele Smith, Elaine McDaid, Marty Clifford and Rachel Blech have been with us since day one. I know, I know, some names are missing here, but to name everybody would mean publishing the Inishowen phone directory!

The biggest boost to the station came in 2001 when ICR secured a FÁS-sponsored Social Economy Project. This meant that

ICR could employ staff to cover a range of essential duties and act as supports to the volunteer members. Many of the staff, including Hugh McGettigan and Brian McGowan, were former volunteers. The project enabled ICR to develop and grow to the stage it is at now, one of the most successful and innovative community stations in the country, with a reputation that stretches far from its secluded location on the edge of the Atlantic. If that sounds boastful, well it's not meant to – it is merely an expression of the pride that we take in what we have achieved to date.

One of these organisations was ADM/CPA which administers the EU Peace II Programme in the border counties. This programme supports ICR's Speak for Yourself! project which aims to address the legacy of the conflict in Inishowen and take advantage of the opportunities arising from peace. A project co-ordinator was appointed in 2002 and since then the project has provided radio training courses to over 100 volunteers at the station, facilitated the expansion of the broadcasting schedule, and provided quality documentary programming focusing on peace projects around the border counties. As well as aiding the peace and reconciliation process in the northwest, Speak for Yourself! has also made a significant financial contribution to the running of ICR and placed the station in a position where it is now regarded as a key player in the area of conflict resolution.

In the few short years that it has existed, ICR has carved out a strong identity for itself both within the northwest and much further afield. The station has been very involved with the national organisation, CRAOL (see Chapter 4), and has been to the forefront of developments in the Irish community radio sector. The station realises that while it has to serve and reflect its own local community, it also has to take a much more outward focus to ensure the proper development of the station. Its home may be the Inishowen peninsula but, as the ICR slogan says, "We may be Peninsular, but we're not Insular!" The station has several overseas projects on the go at any one time and while these sometimes contribute to the station's funds, their true importance lies in other areas. ICR is devoted to promoting the Inishowen region in any way it can and tourism is one of the few growth industries in the area. ICR has been very successful in delivering a positive image of the place abroad and at any one time has several interns from the US, Canada, Australia, Europe and Africa working at the station.

While ICR concentrates on local issues in its programme output, it has developed strong links with NGOs, media organisations and educational institutions from abroad. These include NPR (United States), Euroquest (Radio Netherlands), the Gregorian University (Rome) and St Thomas University (Canada). This has an impact on the station's schedule – you are as likely to hear a report from a refugee camp in Darfur as the latest sheep prices in the local mart. Or even better, those sheep prices being reported by an intern from Los Angeles! We have begun to cater for people newly arrived in the community, for example with a bilingual show presented by a Chinese woman and by developing links leading to programmes by and for the Polish community.

ICR has earned an enviable reputation for itself both within Ireland and abroad for the quality of its programmes and media training, the role that it plays in community development and the strength of its roots within the local community. This did not happen by accident but is due to the committed work and efforts of everyone involved with the station. So long as that commitment is there, then so too will ICR be here for all of the people who live on the peninsula of Inishowen.

18

Going On Air: West Limerick 102

Ciarán Ryan

""Welcome to West Limerick 102, live on air." A huge cheer rang out from volunteers, staff and friends around the station's studios in Newcastle West when volunteer, Eileen O'Sullivan, spoke those words at 4.00 pm on Sunday 15 May 2005. Finally, West Limerick had its own radio station. For me, it marked the end of almost nine months working to help get the station up and running. For others, the process went back a bit further.

With a noticeable void in radio programming focusing on the West Limerick area, a couple of pirate stations began emerging in different pockets of this wide catchment area. A number of people involved in these stations had always wanted to be involved in a licensed radio station, and a steering committee was established to bring community radio to West Limerick. With the assistance of West Limerick Resources, the local LEADER company, a successful application was put forward to the BCI for a temporary one-month broadcast licence during June 2003. Forty volunteers and 460 contributors featured on programming that covered areas such as farming, youth affairs, music, sports, history and much more. The public's reaction was enough to encourage the committee to push for a full broadcasting licence, and a subsequent submission was drafted. I had read with some interest about this station through articles in local papers and had my first encounter with a representative of the station at a CRAOL meeting in Dublin in December 2003.

I had been involved in community radio since 1999. As a student in Mary Immaculate College, University of Limerick, the first port of call was the Wired Fm studio in the library building. Starting as a volunteer who did a *What It Says in the Papers* slot, I went on to work at every level in the station from volunteer presenter with my own music show to paid studio manager on my off-campus year, ending up in deputising as station manager for seven months. When I finally left Wired Fm and college, I was on the job hunt and I saw the West Limerick crew back in the local papers but this time in a different section – Appointments. I applied immediately and, after a successful interview, I was appointed as the Training and Development Officer of West Limerick Community Radio, or West Limerick 102 as it would become known.

When I took up my post at the end of August, the station did not have studios, a transmission network or any of the technical elements that are essential to the running of any kind of radio station. However, it did have a strong core of committed and enthusiastic volunteers who were willing to put the work in and wait for everything else to transpire. While there had been initial plans to have the station up and running by the end of the year, it soon became obvious that this was not feasible. There was a long hard winter ahead with much of the volunteers' time taken up with fundraising. While it built up a sense of camaraderie amongst the volunteers, the picture was not always rosy, like when volunteers got soaked through doing church-gate collections in the pouring rain. Fortunately, throughout all of this, the goodwill of the people of West Limerick undoubtedly assisted in keeping West Limerick Community Radio's volunteers enthusiastic about the project.

After the Christmas holidays, it was down to serious business. Over the previous months, I had met with a huge number of people who were interested in volunteering with the station. Some had been involved in the pilot project, others had come to various meetings that were held or had helped on the fundraising side. Still more had heard about the station through friends or the thousands of newsletters that were circulated throughout the area. They came with a wide range of interests and ranged in age from the mid-teens to the mid-seventies. Of course, people had all kinds of reasons for volunteering – some wanted to build up skills and experience, some were seeking an outlet for self-expression, many wanted to get involved in a community project, a few saw potential career prospects in being in the station and some people just wanted to get to meet new people. Refreshingly, and perhaps one of the reasons why I love working in community radio, everyone who had volunteered did so because they wanted to. It was seen as interesting, stimulating and, most of all, fun.

In January 2005, the first of our training groups started on a cold Monday night. I wouldn't be surprised if I was more anxious about the whole thing than the new trainees who were to come in. Ten people were to start that night, with three other groups to start later that week. I was pleasantly surprised that everyone actually turned up. To any outsider looking in at the first sessions, you would hardly have been able to tell that these people were receiving broadcasting training. Training was not taking place in studios, as they were still being constructed, but instead at the boardroom of West Limerick Resources (WLR). WLR had been instrumental in securing major capital and training funding for the station, as was the local Gaelscoil, who were eager to get involved with the station. We persevered and over the next ten weeks these trainees would receive comprehensive training and we were in a position to start more training groups as the weeks went on. Dan Collins, originally from West Limerick and a former RTÉ producer and founder of Radio Kerry, was heavily involved in the pilot project of 2003. Collins, who had offered me great assistance and advice in my first few months with the station, was responsible for delivering training.

Meanwhile, there was other work to be done. Schools and various community groups were visited. Public meetings were held in most of the different towns and villages scattered around West Limerick. From previous occasions, we knew that people were not overly fond of attending meetings, so we built in a workshop element to entice possible community contributors. The meetings were, for the most part, a success in that a good crowd usually showed up. Better than that, those who came to the meetings showed real interest in the project and committed to contributing to the station when we would go on air. On the down side, there were the instances when windy, narrow back roads were travelled in dark and wet conditions to find that only a couple of people had turned up.

In March 2005 we were able to start holding some of the training sessions in the new studios for the first time. Some new members of staff were brought in, and we finally moved into our offices in April. Tentative on-air dates had been set and passed. Luckily, as paperwork is not my thing, I had no involvement in contract negotiations but I can report that realms of paper were used to ensure each fine detail was in order. The date was finally set for Monday, 9 May 2005. Michael J. Noonan, chairperson of the board, and Mary Kelly, vice-chairperson, travelled to Dublin to meet the BCI and sign the contracts which would allow us to go on air. Just after 5.00 pm, we got word from station manager Diarmuid McIntyre that we were now a licensed station.

The following day was a gloriously sunny one. I was in the town of Abbeyfeale, in our outreach studio, with a group of transition year students from St Joseph's Secondary School who were putting the finishing touches to a programme they were making about their trip to the Gaeltacht. On my way back to the office, I scanned my radio and came across a station I had not found before – West Limerick 102. A call back to the office confirmed that we had indeed begun test transmission that morning, without much fanfare, and that we would be doing so right up until launch time on the following Sunday.

In the week leading up to going on-air, everybody pulled their weight to ensure the station could launch as smoothly as possible. Volunteers knuckled down and planned out future programmes and did dry-runs of their live shows. Nights in the office got later and later, and on one particular evening, with hunger getting the best of me, I took a trip down to a local chipper. Hunger was soon replaced by joy and satisfaction when I heard they were playing our test transmission. A call into the office supplies shop the next day (you'd be surprised how much paper you go through in a radio station) confirmed that more and more businesses were switching over to the station prior to us even going on air officially.

All of this was leading up to our launch date of May 15. There was no waking up in a cold sweat and no nightmare about the radio station. In fact, there was another thing preying on my mind that day – neighbouring county Tipperary were playing Limerick in the first round of the Munster Senior Hurling Championship. Being a Tipp man myself I felt it was not the best day to be at the office in Limerick. We convened at the station around two o'clock, after a quick stop to pick up a few bottles of wine and champagne. Volunteers started filtering in soon after. Nobody was quite sure exactly what was going to happen at four o'clock. We knew we were going on air, but with what was another question. Around ten minutes prior to launch time, all was revealed. For the remainder of the day, different volunteers were to come in, play some of their favourite music and talk about the programmes they were going to be working on. I was asked to man the desk for the first two hours, and for the first time since I started reading *What It Says in the Papers* almost six years previously, I could honestly say, I felt nervous. Sure, I had used desks hundreds of time before, but never was it the first time a station would be going live on-air. Thankfully, when Eileen O'Sullivan introduced West Limerick 102 to the listeners all went well, and *I'm a Believer* from The Monkees blasted out loud and clear calling the community of West Limerick to believe in their new community radio station and in themselves.

As volunteers came and went throughout the afternoon, we went to Semple Stadium for regular updates from our man in the press box, Liam Aherne from Newcastle West. Liam is only 21 but had some previous radio experience, and it showed. Listeners were ringing in to commend him for his reports which sounded "as good as you'd hear in any longstanding station". West Limerick is more renowned as footballing country, but they are a people who have a great interest and pride in their sport, regardless of code. I was in a fairly precarious position, as first Tipp led and I couldn't show my joy in too boisterous a fashion as I knew it could come back to bite me. Pride was resting on this, as indeed were a few euro put down in various bets with volunteers. As Limerick surged ahead in the second half, a few friendly jibes were sent into the studio. Tipp edged back in with a late goal, and when we went to Liam for his final report, Limerick got a last-second equaliser. For some strange reason, I was glad. There was to be no gloating from either side and we got on with the business of broadcasting.

As the long day turned into night, the party outside the studios fizzled out and volunteers trickled back to their homes. The last few people were leaving the station at around 10.00 pm when we got two calls from volunteers alerting us to a major fire in our community midway between the villages of Ballingarry and Knockaderry. It was at that moment, after all the months of training, meetings, paperwork, and even arguments, that it really hit home to us all that this was a real radio station. West Limerick 102 was only a few hours old, and we already had our first breaking news story, before any other local or national station knew about it, all because we had excellent, trained volunteers on the ground. We stayed for a few hours at the station, as volunteer Greg Noonan rang in reports from the scene. Sometime after midnight, and knowing that I had to be at work at 7.30 am the following morning, I knew it was time for sleep and off home I went.

Appendix

AMARC Europe Charter, Adopted Ljubljana, 1994

Recognising that community radio is an ideal means of fostering freedom of expression and information, the development of culture, the freedom to form and confront opinions and active participation in local life; noting that different cultures and traditions lead to diversity of forms of community radio; this Charter identifies objectives which community radio stations share and should strive to achieve.

Community Radio stations:

1. promote the right to communicate, assist the free flow of information and opinions, encourage creative expression and contribute to the democratic process and a pluralist society;

2. provide access to training, production and distribution facilities; encourage local creative talent and foster local traditions; and provide programmes for the benefit, entertainment, education and development of their listeners;

3. seek to have their ownership representative of local geographically recognisable communities or of communities of common interest;

4. are editorially independent of government, commercial and religious institutions and political parties in determining their programming policy;

5. provide a right of access to minority and marginalised groups and promote and protect cultural and linguistic diversity;

6. seek to honestly inform their listeners on the basis of information drawn from a diversity of sources and provide a right of reply to any person or organisation subject to serious misrepresentation;

7. are established as organisations which are not run with a view to profit and ensure their independence by being financed from a variety of sources;

8. recognise and respect the contribution of volunteers, recognise the right of paid workers to join trade unions and provide satisfactory working conditions for both;

9. operate management, programming and employment practices which oppose discriminations and which are open and accountable to all supporters, staff and volunteers;

10. foster exchange between community radio broadcasters using communications to develop greater understanding in support of peace, tolerance, democracy and development.

See website: http://www.amarc.org

Appendix 2

Acronyms

AMARC – French acronym for World Association of Community Broadcasters

AMARC Europe – European branch of World Association of Community Broadcasters

BCI – Broadcasting Commission of Ireland

CAN – Community Action Network, Ireland

CE – Community Employment scheme operated by FÁS

CRAOL – Community Radio Forum of Ireland, not an acronym, uses the Irish word "to broadcast"

CRF – Community Radio Forum of Ireland

CCR – Connemara Community Radio

CRC Fm – Community Radio Castlebar

CRSS – Community Radio Support Scheme

CRY – Community Radio Youghal

DCI – Development Co-operation Ireland

DCU – Dublin City University

DSCR – Dublin South Community Radio

DWR – Dundalk Weekend Radio

FÁS – State Training and Employment Authority

FETAC – Further Education and Training Accreditation Council

FLIRT – Student Community Radio Galway, not an acronym

IBI – Independent Broadcasters of Ireland

ICR – Inishowen Community Radio

IRDL – Inishowen Rural Development Council

IRTC – Independent Radio and Television Commission

ISDN – Integrated Services Digital Network

ITTD – Irish Institute of Training and Development

JNLR – Joint National Radio Listenership Survey

MAMA – Metro Éireann Media and Multi Cultural Awards

NACB – National Association of Community Radio Broadcasters

NALA – National Adult Literacy Agency

NEAR – North East Access Radio

NFP – Northside Folklore Project, Cork city

NGO – Non Government Organisation

NPR – National Public Radio, USA

NUI, Galway – National University of Ireland, Galway

NWCI – National Women's Council of Ireland

NWCR – North West Community Radio

OB – Outside Broadcast

OBU – Outside Broadcasting Unit

PACE – Prisoners' Aid through Community Effort

RCB – Radio Corca Baiscinn

RTC – Regional Technical College

RTÉ – Raidió Teilifís Éireann

TCR – Tallaght Community Radio

TD – *Teachta Dála,* member of Irish parliament, lower house

VEC – Vocational Education Committee

UCC – University College Cork

UCD – University College Dublin

UCG – University College Galway

WDAR – West Dublin Access Radio

WDCR – West Dublin Community Radio

References

ADM, 1991. Area Development Management. http://www.adm.ie

Alinsky, S, 1971. *Rules for Radicals: A Practical Primer for Realistic Radicals.* London: Random House.

Baehr, H. (ed.) 1980. *Women and Media.* New York: Pergammon Press.

BCI, 2000. *Training and Development Policy.* Dublin: BCI.

BCI, 2002, BCI *Community Radio Policy*, Dublin: BCI.

BCI, 2003, *Nathanna Cainte don Raidió.* Dublin: BCI.

Brecht, B., 1930. "Radio as a Means of Communication: A Talk on the Functions of Radio". In Mattelart, A. and S. Siegelaub (eds.). 1983. *Communication and Class Struggle: 2.* New York/Bagnolet: International General & IMMRC. 169-171.

CCR, 1994. Application to the IRTC for Community Radio License to Broadcast. Unpublished.

Chomsky, N. and E. Herman, 1988. *Manufacturing Consent: Political Economy of the Mass Media.* New York: Pantheon.

Day, R., 2003. *Community Radio in Ireland: Participation, Building the Community, Multi-flows of Communication.* Unpublished PhD Thesis, Dublin City University.

Day, R., 2007. *Community Radio in Ireland: Participation and Multi-flows of Communication.* Cresskill, NJ: Hampton Press.

Day, R., 2007. *An Droichead: Lámhleabhar Traenála Raidió.* Dublin: BCI.

Dillon, B. and S. Ó Siochrú, 1997. *IRTC Pilot Community Radio Stations: Evaluation Workshops: Final Report.* Dublin: Nexus Co-operative.

Enzensberger, H.M., 1970. "Constituents of a Theory of the Media". In: Roloff, M. (ed.), 1974. *Hans Magnus Enzensberger: The Consciousness Industry, On Literature, Politics and the Media.*

Freire, P., 1970. *Pedagogy of the Oppressed.* New York: Herder and Herder.

Gibbons, M., 1998. *Breaking Glass Walls: Gender and Employment Issues in the Independent Radio Sector in Ireland.* Dublin: Nexus Co-operative.

Girard, B., 1992. *Passion for Radio.* Montreal: Black Rose Books.

Habermas, J., 1983. *The Structural Transformation of the Public Sphere: An Inquiry into a Category of Bourgeois Society.* Cambridge: Polity Press.

Hall, S., 1993. "Culture, Community, Nation". In: *Cultural Studies* 7/3: 349-363.

IPU, 2006. *InterParliamentary Union.* www.ipu.org

IRTC, 1997. *IRTC Community Radio Policy.* Dublin: IRTC.

IRTC, 2000. *Nathanna Cainte don Raidió.* Dublin: IRTC.

IRTC, 2001. *Irish Language Broadcasting in the Independent Sector.* Dublin: IRTC.

Kelleher, P. and M. Whelan, 1992. *Dublin Communities in Action.* Dublin: CAN/Combat Poverty Agency.

Lewis, P.M., 1989. *The Invisible Medium: Public, Commercial and Community Radio.* London: Macmillan Press.

Lippmann, W., 1922. *Public Opinion.* Salt Lake City: Project Gutenberg. http://www.projectgutenberg.com

McGann, N., 2003. *The Empowerment of Women through Participation in Community Radio.* Unpublished MA Thesis, Mary Immaculate College, University of Limerick.

McSkeanne, L., 1999. *Literacy through the Airwaves: A Radio Project for Adults – Project Evaluation Report.* Dublin: National Adult Literacy Agency.

Mulryan, P., 1989. *Radio, Radio.* Dublin: Borderline Productions.

NWCI, 2006. National Women's Council of Ireland Publications, http://www.nwci.ie

Salter, L., 1980. "Two Directions on a One Way Street: Old and New Approaches in Media Analysis in Two Decades". In: *Studies in Communication* 1: 85-117.

Unique Perspectives, 2003. *Community Radio in Ireland: Its Contribution to Community Development.* Dublin: CRAOL.

WDCR, 1994. Application to the IRTC for Community Radio License to Broadcast. Unpublished.